The Joy of Being Retired

The Joy of Being Retired

**365 REASONS WHY RETIREMENT ROCKS
— AND WORK SUCKS!**

Ernie J. Zelinski

Visions International Publishing

Direct any inquiries about foreign rights and quantity purchases to:

Visions International Publishing

P.O. Box 4072

Edmonton, Alberta, Canada, T6E 4S8

Phone (780) 434-9202

E-mail: vip-books@telus.net

The Joy of Being Retired: 365 Reasons Why Retirement Rocks — and Works Sucks!

ISBN: 978-1-927452-04-2

Printed in Canada

*Dedicated to All the Happy Retirees and All the Wannabes Who
Still Love the Concept of Retirement*

Other Life-Changing Books by Ernie J. Zelinski

The Joy of Not Working: A Book for the Retired, Unemployed, and Overworked (over 310,000 copies sold and published in 17 languages)

How to Retire Happy, Wild, and Free: Retirement Wisdom That You Won't Get from Your Financial Advisor (over 390,000 copies sold and published in 10 languages)

The Lazy Person's Guide to Success: How to Get What You Want Without Killing Yourself for It (over 110,000 copies sold and published in 11 languages)

Look Ma, Life's Easy: How Ordinary People Attain Extraordinary Success and Remarkable Prosperity

Life's Secret Handbook: Reminders for Adventurous Souls Who Want to Make a Big Difference in This World

Career Success Without a Real Job: The Career Book for People Too Smart to Work in Corporations

101 Really Important Things You Already Know, But Keep Forgetting (Over 50,000 copies sold and published in 10 languages)

"If I'd known that retirement was going to be this good,
I'd have done it the day after I left school!"
— Mickey White

INTRODUCTION

THERE WAS A TIME WHEN the word "retirement" was joyfully expressed and thought by the majority to be a special phase of a person's life. Retirement has been getting a bad name lately, however, particularly from people who don't have a clue about how to enjoy themselves with all their free time. A little sad, wouldn't you say?

No doubt even during the best of times the fallout from retirement can be good or not so good, depending on the type of individual you are and what your financial status is when you retire. In this book I am focusing on the positive aspects of retirement. There are many.

The great news is that studies show that a lot more people enjoy retirement than those who don't. The purpose of *The Joy of Being Retired* is to help you join the group of individuals who are truly happy to be retired.

Some of the more interesting benefits of retirement cited in this book come from individuals other than me, including those who have written letters to me after reading my two international bestselling retirement books *How to Retire Happy, Wild, and Free* and *The Joy of Not Working*.

Like me, many people are not big fans of having to work in the typical corporation. This is what makes retirement so special. Regardless of how terrible your workplace may have been, the important thing is to have a happy and prosperous retirement — because millions of creative and optimistic individuals are experiencing a great retirement!

"One day you will wake up and there won't be any more time to do the things you've always wanted," warned Brazilian writer Paulo Coelho. "Do it now." With that in mind, here are 365 reasons why retirement rocks — and work sucks! Actually, that's not quite true. As it turns out, there is no off-switch on this genius machine. I couldn't stop at 365 reasons once I got wound up. I had to wind down with 50 bonus reasons for a total of 415 reasons why retirement rocks — and work sucks!

Regardless of the bad press that retirement gets nowadays, there has never been a better time to be retired. My wish is that this book serves as an important reminder why you left the workplace in the first place. Above all, I hope that this book along with my two other retirement books help make retirement the best time of your life.

365 Reasons Why Retirement Rocks – and Work Sucks!

Why Retirement Rocks – Reason #1

Retirement allows you to pursue your first love which is living life to the fullest! A truly satisfying and happy retirement includes interesting leisure activities, creative pursuits, physical well-being, mental well-being, a defined sense of purpose, and a great sense of community.

Why Retirement Rocks – Reason #2

In retirement you will realize that living at work just to get by was not enough. Just like the butterfly, an adventurous soul needs a varied and enchanting life — green grass and happy skies, freedom to go where it pleases, and joys that await it.

Why Retirement Rocks — Reason #3

Harry Mahtar remarked, "A gold watch is the most appropriate gift for retirement, as its recipients have given up so many of their golden hours in a lifetime of service." By having retired early, you don't have to wind up like so many people who retire too late — they have given so much of themselves to their companies that they don't have anything left in the tank to enjoy their retirement years. You do!

Why Retirement Rocks — Reason #4

You get to appreciate one of life's great pleasures — lots of time on your hands. That means exchanging a grueling nine-to-five routine for a well-earned casual and carefree lifestyle. You can pay attention to — and follow — the good advice that comes unexpectedly. For example, the menu in a Canadian restaurant advises:

"If you're not served in 5 minutes, you'll be served in 8 or 9 . . . . Maybe 12 minutes.

RELAX!"

Why Retirement Rocks — Reason #5

If you don't feel like doing anything serious at all except lounging around your apartment — that's exactly what you get to do. As famous American writer Louise Beebe Wilder pointed out, "He [she] lacks much who has no aptitude for idleness."

Why Retirement Rocks — Reason #6

"Life may not be the party we hoped for," stated some unknown wise person, "but while we are here we should dance." Being retired means that you can go dancing until 4 AM on a weeknight and not have to worry about going to work the next day.

Why Retirement Roks – Reason #7

Here is the typical "worker's dilemma": No matter how much you do, you will never have done enough. Of course, what you have done is never "good" enough. Furthermore, what you didn't do due to a lack of time is always more important than what you did do. The act of early retirement solves this unrelenting and dejecting dilemma.

Why Retirement Rocks – Reason #8

You can play golf every day of the week. In spring, your spouse and you can be the first people on the course while the working stiffs wait for summer vacation to spend sufficient time on the course.

Why Retirement Rocks – Reason #9

If a Meyer-Briggs professional personality assessment test given by your employer indicated that you were best suited for retirement, you can now put your skills and talent to good use.

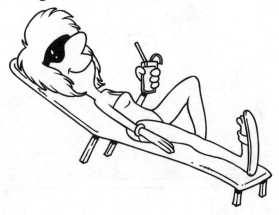

Why Retirement Rocks – Reason #10

Your cat and dog don't have to be lonely on weekdays because you are no longer at the workplace. In fact, they get to enjoy your retirement even more than you. The act of spending more time with animals that adore you and like to have fun with you will improve your emotional outlook on life.

Why Retirement Rocks – Reason #11

No more nightmares about the workload that will await you when you arrive at work in the morning.

Why Retirement Rocks – Reason #12

You get to take your dog for a walk three times a day. Better said, your dog gets to take you for a walk three times a day. That's a good thing for you, however, since the great deal of exercise will do you a lot of good. Research shows that the simple act of walking your dog will boost your fitness level, increase social activity, and give your sense of well-being a boost.

Why Retirement Rocks — Reason #13

Working long hours can sometimes be rewarding, without doubt, but so can goofing off and enjoying life. As they say in Spain, "How nice it is to do nothing all day and then rest afterward." Clearly, hard work doesn't lead to happiness. If hard work guaranteed happiness, over  90 percent of all Americans would be truly happy. Surprisingly, psychologists and psychiatrists say that only about 20 percent of the total population is happy.

Why Retirement Rocks — Reason #14

 When you take early retirement from a stressful job, you immediately look about seventeen years younger — simply because you feel about seventeen years younger. Moreover, when you get to love yourself immensely more just for having made the decision to retire early, you look younger without even trying.

7

Why Retirement Rocks – Reason #15

You can wake up in the morning with nothing to do and by bedtime be in a position of having done only half of it — with no major consequences. "The time you enjoy wasting," advised famous Canadian educator Laurence J. Peter, "is not wasted time."

Why Retirement Rocks – Reason #16

With your new found freedom that retirement brings, you no longer have to play for safety — because as Hugh Walpole pointed out, "it's the most dangerous thing in the world."

Why Retirement Rocks — Reason #17

You get to restore the classic car that you purchased in your thirties, which you drove into the ground, and that is still sitting in your garage waiting to be restored to look like it looked when it was brand new.

Why Retirement Rocks — Reason #18

Perhaps at work you were a fly stuck in a thick tar of despair and to lots of post-it notes. The gross incompetence of your co-workers hung heavily in the air like the cold stench of a bunch of dead fish. Even more than your co-workers, you longed for the comfort of a grave. Eventually your job convinced you that work life was a stale joke with absolutely no punch line. This situation may not have given rise to the level of an international crisis — but it did carry an extreme amount of stress and emotional damage. Viva la retirement!

Why Retirement Rocks – Reason #19

Retirement gives you the time and opportunity to happily spend the kids' inheritance, which according to recent studies a lot of current retirees intend to do. As money guru Sandra Block warned us, "Leaving your heirs a big amount of money doesn't guarantee tears at your funeral." In fact, if you want your heirs to cry, ensure that you leave them absolutely nothing.

Why Retirement Rocks – Reason #20

You get to spend a lot more time with your spouse and learn how to compromise, how to pick the right battles, and how not to kill each other. In other words, you get to put your marriage to the ultimate test.

Why Retirement Rocks – Reason #21

Your brain, after being brainwashed by corporate culture for so long, just may be jarred into new ways of creative thinking. Indeed, new perspectives on living are usually fostered when people have more time to reflect and reassess the true meaning of life. *Life's Secret Handbook* suggests, "You may want to be known for your spirit, your creativity, and the difference you make in this world. To be nimble-witted, street smart, and spiritually aware is to abreast of the advanced and magical workings of the universe."

Why Retirement Rocks – Reason #22

No more need to set several alarm clocks! If you were like my friend Forrest Bard who at one time used 25 to 35 alarm clocks to get up on time, then mornings in retirement will seem incredibly peaceful compared to mornings while you were working.

Why Retirement Rocks – Reason #23

You will have attained true freedom in this world when you can get up in the morning when you want to get up; go to sleep when you want to go to sleep; and in the interval, work and play at the things you want to work and play at — all at your own pace. The great news is that retirement allows you the opportunity to attain this freedom.

Why Retirement Rocks – Reason #24

Retirement allows you to make the most of your life in a relaxed manner — knowing that most of your working friends are at work stressed and mentally aching. You can set a relaxing schedule each week instead of a stress-filled one:

- Monday   Comb hair.
- Tuesday   Brush teeth.
- Wednesday   Take a shower.
- Thursday   Clip toe nails.
- Friday   Shave.
- Saturday   Take the dog for a walk.
- Sunday   Put on clean clothes, perhaps.

Why Retirement Rocks — Reason #25

You have all the time in the world to prove The Law of Napping — A Body at Rest Remains at Rest.

Why Retirement Rocks — Reason #26

Mark Twain said, "I shall never use profanity except in discussing house rent and taxes." In retirement, generally speaking, you earn less money with the result that you pay a lot less income tax. And if you have always hated paying income tax, this should make you truly happy.

Why Retirement Rocks — Reason #27

You can now preach the shortcomings of the work ethic and proclaim to the world — as the great philosopher Bertrand Russell once did — that "the morality of work is the morality of slaves and the world has no need for more slavery." Fact is, hard work is the best thing ever invented for killing time – as well as you. The secret to a happy life is to work as hard as you have to for a comfortable living — and as little as you can get away with.

Why Retirement Rocks — Reason #28

A lower retirement income than the income you made when you were working teaches you that there are a lot of things that you can do without — such as the $495 Falke brand name socks that you bought — and still be happy. Besides, you always misplaced those expensive socks and could never find them anyway, right?

Why Retirement Rocks – Reason #29

You always have time to make your bed every weekday morning, unlike during your work years when it remained unmade all week. There are some surprising advantages to making your bed each day such as it starts your day off right, it encourages you to keep the rest of your room tidy, and it just looks and feels better.

Why Retirement Rocks – Reason #30

You can make a top-10 list for each of the things you should do, the things you must do, the things you might do, the things you have seen done, the things you wish you would have done, the things you could do, the things you wanted to do, and the things you have dreamed of doing. This should keep you quite busy for the rest of your retirement days.

Why Retirement Rocks — Reason #31

At least once in your life you should paint a picture — even if it doesn't rank up there with any by artist Pablo Picasso. Retirement is when you get to do this with great flair. "The artist is a receptacle for emotions," said Picasso, "that come from all over the place: from the sky, from the earth, from a scrap of paper, from a passing shape, from a spider's web."

Why Retirement Rocks — Reason #32

You can find the time to experience a multitude of "real adventures" such as visiting a farm to hug a cow or heading to the North Pole to experience how cold it is there. If the North Pole is not cold enough for you, you can always try the South Pole in Antarctica. For the record, Antarctica is the site of the lowest temperature ever recorded on earth, -89.2° C (-128.6° F).

Why Retirement Rocks – Reason #33

You can now have that tattoo made that simply says "Work Sucks — and Retirement Rocks!" Many Millennials, Generation Xers, and even working Baby Boomers will be so envious of you. Do you think that you are too old for a tattoo? London's top tattooists, some who can boast waiting lists of more than two years, now report seeing almost as many 40-80-somethings as they do Millennials. And guess what? The majority of their clients are women.

Why Retirement Rocks – Reason #34

You don't have to act your age in retirement as you do at work; in retirement you can act like the inner young person you have always been. Indeed, you get to find

out that you are never too old to become a little bit younger in spirit. "The idea is to die young, as late as possible," suggested British-American anthropologist Ashley Montagu.

Why Retirement Rocks — Reason #35

You can finally find the time needed to write a scathing exposé of that ruthless bastard-of-a-rat boss for whom you used to have to work. Also, no more of that fat guy in the stupid-looking suit getting all the credit for the great creative work that you did.

Why Retirement Rocks — Reason #36

You no longer have to worry about being laid off and how you are going to break the news to your spouse. The ideal would have been to become irreplaceable so you couldn't get fired for your behavior or because of a bad economy. In retirement you can think of yourself as irreplaceable because you can't be fired for your behavior or because of a bad economy.

Why Retirement Rocks – Reason #37

You get to shop for groceries when most people are at work, which means you can do this at any speed you want. If you must hurry, however, then try to hurry slowly. Speed kills – in more ways than one.

Why Retirement Rocks – Reason #38

Ahhh retirement! Fishing yesterday, fishing today, and fishing tomorrow! What's there not to like about this if you truly love fishing? "If fishing is a religion," declared Tom Brokaw, "fly fishing is high church."

Why Retirement Rocks – Reason #39

Even when the fishing isn't as great as you would like, retirement life is still pretty darn good. There are many other joyful and satisfying things to look forward to for the rest of the day.

Why Retirement Rocks – Reason #40

You have the time to cook and eat the fish the same day that you catch it. Expert fishermen say that there is little to compare with the taste of fish that has been well cared for since capture, especially fish that we have caught ourselves. That is one of the true joys of fishing.

Why Retirement Rocks – Reason #41

Retirement is the time to do the things you intended to do when you were still working — and if you don't do them, who cares? Put another way in the words of Yoshida Kanko, "Retirement is the time to leave undone whatever you hesitate to do."

Why Retirement Rocks – Reason #42

On April 15, 1882 Mark Twain gave an inspirational speech to young people and advised them, "Be respectful to your superiors, if you have any." The great thing about retirement is that you have no superiors. You get to be your own boss all the time.

Why Retirement Rocks — Reason #43

You get to tell all your friends, "If I had known that retirement would be this great, I would have killed to have gotten here sooner." These were, in fact, the words uttered by retiree Kirk Symmes after he was forced to retire from his sales job at sixty-five and took on a part-time fun retirement job as a college instructor.

Why Retirement Rocks — Reason #44

Age, according to Francis Bacon, appears to be best in four things: "Old wood best to burn, old wine to drink, old friends to trust, and old authors to read." Needless to say, regardless of the age at which you retire, you can enjoy all four.

Why Retirement Rocks – Reason #45

You get to toot your own horn about the benefits of retirement. There are many. One of the most important

benefits is the freedom to do what you want. A 2016 Merrill Lynch study found that 92 percent of retirees said that retirement has given them much greater freedom and flexibility to pursue their own interests, irrespective of how much money they have saved.

Why Retirement Rocks – Reason #46

You get to find out that the key to a great retirement is to find joy in little things, such as saying "Hi" to babies in carriages. One important note: Don't joyfully say "bonjour" unless you know that the baby understands French.

Why Retirement Rocks – Reason #47

"Why retire when you're too old to enjoy it? Quit your job now!" stated the headline in the Business Section of the *Los Angeles Times* on August 2, 2018. Andrew Wind, 38, did just that. Three months into his trip, with a year to go, his plans were to visit about 30 countries and 45 cities, finish writing a book, some screenplays and TV pilots, and become conversational in French and Spanish. Of course, this is extremely difficult to accomplish when one is working.

Why Retirement Rocks – Reason #48

When you retire, nothing has to be taken seriously, even aging. As the late US President Abraham Lincoln mentioned, "It's not the years in your life that count. It's the life in your years."

Why Retirement Rocks – Reason #49

Retirement is the time to spend less time with people you dislike — such as some of the co-workers you had to put up with — and much more time with people you truly like regardless of how eccentric they are.

Why Retirement Rocks – Reason #50

You can finally find the time to learn how to play a musical instrument of your choice. Learning to play an instrument increases the capacity of your memory, enhances your coordination, exposes you to cultural history, sharpens your concentration, fosters your self-expression, reduces stress, and promotes happiness in your life and for those people around you.

Why Retirement Rocks – Reason #51

Perhaps you amassed a large collection of cookbooks as have some people, not putting the vast majority of them to good use. Former *Los Angeles Times* food editor Russ Parsons acquired almost 2,000 cookbooks. Better still, Maryellen Burns, author of *The Lost Restaurants of*  *Sacramento – and Their Recipes*, amassed a collection of more than 4,000 cookbooks. Retirement is a great time to put some or all of these cookbooks to good use by doing a lot of Japanese, Thai, Indonesian, Basque, Spanish, Hungarian, etc. cooking. Of course, too many cookbooks are like too many tools in an amateur mechanic's garage. At some point, some of the tools have to go. Retirement is the opportunity to downsize either the collection of tools or the collection of cookbooks by giving some away or by selling them.

Why Retirement Rocks – Reason #52

In retirement you have no problem saving at least one evening a week to spend happily with only your spouse and you.

Why Retirement Rocks — Reason #53

Unlike when you were working at a job, you have the time — and the disposition — to compliment at least three people a day. "Pleasant words are as a honeycomb," advises the *Hebrew Bible*, "sweet to the soul, and health to the bones." Remember that flattery makes great friends — and great friends make up an important ingredient for a happy life.

Why Retirement Rocks — Reason #54

You get to use the good silver a lot more — even if it is just for a barbecue — because you have a lot more time to cook for your friends and relatives. Keep in mind the fine words of author and former restaurateur Alice May Brock:

"Tomatoes and oregano make it Italian; wine and tarragon make it French. Sour cream makes it Russian; lemon and cinnamon make it Greek. Soy sauce makes it Chinese; garlic makes it good."

Why Retirement Rocks — Reason #55

Oh what a great feeling! Truly experiencing a shower every morning for as long as you want — and even singing while having it. Long, warm showers are good for you in more ways than one. Religions and spiritual paths from many parts of the world embrace the healing symbolism of running  water to restore and soothe body, mind and spirit. Indeed, in retirement you have the luxury of having two or even three showers a day and not at all feeling guilty about it.

Why Retirement Rocks — Reason #56

 You no longer have to suppress yourself to the complete forfeiture of experience, being a working drone, utterly inert, caught in a workplace web. Greek philosopher Aristotle emphasized this so well centuries ago when he declared, "All paid jobs absorb and degrade the mind." In contrast, in retirement you have the opportunity to enhance your mind with many new and interesting experiences.

Why Retirement Rocks — Reason #57

You can be busier than ever. If you ask retirees what their lives are like, most will tell you that they are busier than ever before — wondering how they ever had time to go to work. Every day is filled with errands, shopping, household chores, yard work, TV and movies, club meetings, and all sorts of other even much more important things.

Why Retirement Rocks — Reason #58

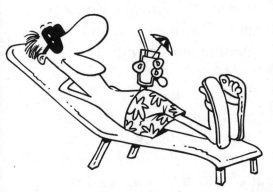

Instead of taking naps restricted to Sunday afternoons, you can take a nap every afternoon of the week, or when the urge hits. The Sleep Foundation reports that "more than 85 percent of mammalian species are polyphasic sleepers, meaning that they sleep for short periods throughout the day. While naps do not necessarily make up for inadequate or poor quality nighttime sleep, a short nap of 20-30 minutes can help to improve mood, alertness, and performance."

Why Retirement Rocks – Reason #59

As a retired woman, you have all the time in the world to join the Red Hat Society (RHS). The RHS (www.redhatsociety.com) is comprised of women from all walks of life who are committed to joyful living, growing, exploring new interests, having fun, and meeting new friends.

Why Retirement Rocks – Reason #60

Retirement is a time to learn and identify the music of Chopin, Mozart, and Beethoven. Without mentioning Chopin, Henri-Frédéric Amiel stated, "Mozart has the classic purity of light and the blue ocean; Beethoven the romantic grandeur which belongs to the storms of air and sea, and while the soul of Mozart seems to dwell on the ethereal peaks of Olympus, that of Beethoven climbs shuddering the storm-beaten sides of a Sinai. Blessed be they both! Each represents a moment of the ideal life, each does us good. Our love is due to both."

Why Retirement Rocks – Reason #61

You can finally get around to writing a book. Here are ten non-financial reasons to write a book in retirement:

- Writing a book will get you out of your comfort zone.
- You will learn new skills and keep your mind in shape.
- You will develop more curiosity and be more open to new ideas.
- You get to share your unique message with the world.
- You will feel a great sense of accomplishment when it is finally completed – because it is a lot of work.
- When you hold your book in your hand, you've beaten the odds. A little over 85 percent of adults want to write a book – only 5 percent do!
- You can have a big celebration when you finish the book and give copies to friends, relatives, and even strangers.
- You will get more respect from others.
- You get to meet a lot of interesting people by having your book with you at all times.
- You will leave a legacy to your children and grandchildren because your book is something tangible and long lasting.

Why Retirement Rocks — Reason #62

Being retired means that you can try to attain the "Top-Ten Travel Goals" people chose on a well-know travel website:

1. Travel the world.
2. See the northern lights.
3. Go on a road trip with no predetermined destination.
4. Visit all 50 states.
5. Backpack through Europe.
6. Go on a cruise.
7. Go on a road trip.
8. Sleep under the stars.
9. Visit another country.
10. Leave my city once a month

Why Retirement Rocks – Reason #63

Truth be told, work kills more than war. Approximately two million workers die annually due to occupational injuries and illnesses, according to a United Nations report. This is more than double the figure for deaths from warfare (650,000 deaths per year). If you like to toy with death, work is okay. If not, retirement is the only intelligent alternative.

Why Retirement Rocks – Reason #64

Retirement life allows you to slow down and show some sanity while driving your car. There is no need to speed. "This is where our obsession with going fast and saving time leads," says Carl Honoré, author of *In Praise of Slowness*. "To road rage, air rage, shopping rage, relationship rage, office rage, vacation rage, gym rage. Thanks to speed, we live in the age of rage." In short, retirement can eliminate all this repressed rage.

Why Retirement Rocks – Reason #65

You can finally find the time to teach your dog a few new tricks such as how to play soccer with you. Ten other tricks that you can teach your dog are to kiss you on command, bark on command, shake hands, fetch, roll over, play dead, spin, stand on its hind legs, sit pretty, and to hug you. Check the Dog Time website (www.dogtime.com) for more details.

Why Retirement Rocks – Reason #66

Ever notice how fast all those warm summer days slip by, particularly when you have to spend eight to ten hours a day at a job? Being retired allows you to appreciate each one of those summer days to the fullest, at a Café or wherever, as if each was a gift from Heaven just for you.

Why Retirement Rocks – Reason #67

Retirement is the time to take a photography course and take some great creative photos of friends, children, grandchildren, and landscapes. Photography is more than just a hobby or a vocation. It is a way to express your self, to capture the diverse moments that string together the flow of life, and a way to preserve these moments for life.

Why Retirement Rocks – Reason #68

Once you retire, you no longer have to hear these depressing words from relatives, friends and co-workers, "Hang in there, retirement is only ten to twenty years away!" When you experience retirement fully, you get to achieve remarkable personal growth and higher consciousness, two elements of happiness and satisfaction that are  difficult to experience in the typical workplace.

Why Retirement Rocks — Reason #69

Retirement is the time you truly realize that happiness is not based on possessions, power, and prestige — but on relationships with people who you deeply love and respect.

Why Retirement Rocks — Reason #70

Retirement is also the time to whistle a happy tune every day. This is pretty hard to do when you have to go to work every day. You can even try to master "The 15 Best Whistling Songs of All Time" according to *Rolling Stone* magazine. These include 'Patience,' by Guns N' Roses, 'Dock of the Bay' by Otis Redding, 'Don't Worry, Be Happy' by Bobby McFerrin, and 'White Christmas' by Bing Crosby.

Why Retirement Rocks — Reason #71

Working life is when you judge your success by promotions, salary, and raises; retirement is when you judge your success by the degree that you are enjoying peace, health, love, and your dog.

Why Retirement Rocks — Reason #72

Being retired affords you the time to learn how to make something truly artistic and beautiful with your hands, even if this means painting a computer keyboard. Recall Abraham Maslow, the American psychologist and a co-founder of humanistic psychology who developed a hierarchical model of human motivation, in which a higher need, ultimately one for self-actualization, is expressed only after lower needs are fulfilled. Maslow rightfully observed, "A musician must make music, an artist must paint, a poet must write, if he [she] is to be ultimately at peace with himself [herself]."

Why Retirement Rocks — Reason #73

Retirement is the perfect time to forget about keeping up with the Joneses and other neighbors, who are highly influenced by advertisers to spend money on worthless stuff and wind up in debt big time.

Why Retirement Rocks — Reason #74

You can take a whole year to read *War and Peace* from cover to cover — and any other books that you should have read a long time ago. For a much shorter book try *The Little Prince* by Antoine de Saint Exupéry. Aside from the *Bible*, this book is the most translated book ever with it being translated into 300 languages. The second most translated book ever is *Pinocchio* by Carlo Collodi with 260 languages but, of course, they could be lying about this one.

Why Retirement Rocks — Reason #75

Retirement life means being able to think big thoughts — and then discard them to relish small pleasures, instead. E.A. Bucchianeri stated, "Sometimes, the simple things are more fun and meaningful than all the banquets in the world." In the same vein, Walt Whitman said that "A morning-glory at my window satisfies me more than the metaphysics of books."

Why Retirement Rocks — Reason #76

No more of the multi-tasking that was imposed on you at your workplace. In 2009 Clifford Nass, a professor at Stanford University, set out to find out how well so-called "multitaskers" multitasked. After an extensive study he found that "High multitaskers are suckers for irrelevancy," along with "Multitaskers were just lousy at everything." As Steve Uzzell pointed out, "Multitasking is merely the opportunity to screw up more than one thing at a time." Fortunately, once you retire you don't have to indulge in this craziness called "workplace multi-tasking" anymore.

Why Retirement Rocks — Reason #77

As a retiree who wants to give to your community, you get to choose a charity and support it generously with your time, effort, and money. Working for a charity creates feelings of growth, achievement, responsibility, and recognition. The result is a sense of  satisfaction and happiness that no amount of money can ever buy. American comedian and civil rights activist Dick Gregory agreed when he reflected about his life and said, "One of the things I keep learning is that the secret of being happy is doing things for other people."

Why Retirement Rocks — Reason #78

Retirement is the time to be bold and courageous. "Twenty years from now you will be more disappointed by the things you didn't do than by the ones you did do," suggested Mark Twain. "So throw off the bowlines. Sail away from the safe harbor. Catch the trade winds in your sails. Explore. Dream. Discover."

Why Retirement Rocks – Reason #79

No more commuting to work means less driving and much less of a chance of your doing a number on your car (and someone else's).

Why Retirement Rocks – Reason #80

You can finally find the time to take a martial arts course such as aikido, karate, tae kwon do, or judo to

defend yourself from potential human-inflicted injury. Of course, other benefits of martial arts courses are a strong and powerful physical body, improved flexibility, improved stability and coordination, lower blood pressure and heart rate, mental concentration, and stress relief.

Why Retirement Rocks – Reason #81

Retirement can be the time for you to become the most positive and enthusiastic person you know. This will help you age gracefully. A study conducted in the USA confirms that people who have a positive outlook on life live longer and look younger than people who have a negative outlook on life.

Why Retirement Rocks – Reason #82

Retirement gives you all the time in the world to engage in the art of conversation. If you are negative, you can talk endlessly to others about life, certainly about how it is pointless, the cruelty of man, and the stupidity of all politicians. On the other hand, if you are a Pollyanna, you can talk forever and a day about non-duality, how the time is coming soon when we will all have shed our egos, we will all have a divine unity with each other, and we will all love Donald Trump, while Donald at the same time will have nothing but great things to say about each of us (except about me, of course).

Why Retirement Rocks – Reason #83

Retirement is the time to reread your favorite books.

Why Retirement Rocks – Reason #84

Bonnie Ware, an Australian palliative nurse, recorded the most common regrets of the dying. The top five:

1. I wish I'd had the courage to live a life true to myself, not the life others expected of me.
2. I wish I hadn't worked so hard.
3. I wish I'd had the courage to express my feelings.
4. I wish I had stayed in touch with my friends.
5. I wish that I had let myself be happier.

Early retirement gives you the opportunity to live out your life with much gusto and swagger so that your epitaph can read, "No Regrets!"

Why Retirement Rocks — Reason #85

You can start the retirement internet business that you have wanted to start and get corporate sponsorships to pay for your annual winter vacations in Hawaii. Better still, you can move to Hawaii and run your business there.

Why Retirement Rocks — Reason #86

As the *Washington Post* reported in 2017, one of the most universal — and universally hated — things we do is waiting in line. Altogether, some people spend a year or two of their lives waiting in line, estimates Richard Larson, a professor who studies queuing theory at MIT. In  retirement, you seldom have to stand in line, even in grocery stores, because you have a lot more flexibility in regards to when you do those things that can end up making you stand in line.

Why Retirement Rocks – Reason #87

When you wake up and see that it is a gorgeous morning, the daily drudgery of making a living no longer has to interfere with your enjoying the morning. You can just go out and enjoy it. "If you retire right the only thing you will worry about is when to eat and when to sleep," concluded an unknown wise person.

Why Retirement Rocks – Reason #88

You can always take the scenic route when you are retired — regardless of where you are going — just like you did when you were a hippy in the 1960s. Taking the scenic route can become a new healthy routine. You have two choices: the fastest and most direct route to your  destination, or "the scenic route," the longer and slower path that allows you to relax and enjoy the trip. Before mass airplane travel, the train was how many vacation tours were accomplished, helping the term get established. Taking the scenic route means the stress of driving melts away and you realize you've made the right choice by adding a little time to your drive. You took the scenic route, and you couldn't be happier about it.

Why Retirement Rocks — Reason #89

"That so few now dare to be eccentric, marks the chief danger of the time," warned John Stuart Mill. In this regard, you will have a much easier go around in life when you stop following the herd. Your chances for a full, relaxed, satisfying, and happy life will tend to increase in direct proportion to how much you are out of step with the rest of society. Certainly, the more unconventional and eccentric you are, the better. Retirement life allows you to be as eccentric as you would like to be.

Why Retirement Rocks — Reason #90

You no longer have to appraise your friends and acquaintances using the "work ethic" as a measuring tool. Now you can use the "play ethic" as the most important tool for evaluating the individuals who associate with you.

Why Retirement Rocks — Reason #91

Life in retirement is more exciting because as an innovative person you can create excitement in your

leisure activities and don't have to be constrained by a staid and controlling workplace. When it's 2 o'clock in the afternoon on a work day, the sun is shining, and you're itching to spend the rest of the afternoon outdoors, this is exactly what you do — unlike corporate workers who have to spend their time imprisoned in a cubicle, working at a lousy job.

Why Retirement Rocks — Reason #92

In the typical workplace you can be fired for being politically incorrect. When you are retired, if you get thrown out of a favorite coffee bar for making unpopular comments, you can always find a funkier coffee bar with more open-minded people in which to hang out. You can also wear your TGiF (Thank God it's Friday) T-shirt every day of the week in whatever coffee bar you choose to hang out.

Why Retirement Rocks – Reason #93

You can be the person who returns acceptance and dignity to the art of loafing.

Why Retirement Rocks – Reason #94

Because you are now a truly free person, you get to feel light as a feather every day.

Why Retirement Rocks — Reason #95

Henry David Thoreau advocated that "Simplicity, simplicity, simplicity!" is the key to a happy life. In retirement you can "simplify, simplify, simplify" your affairs — and lead a much happier life.

Why Retirement Rocks — Reason #96

The Declaration of Independence provides every American the right of the pursuit of happiness. Problem is, most Americans have been pursuing happiness madly through work and money. The more they have desperately pursued happiness, the more elusive it has become. In retirement you get to realize that the way to happiness is to slow down and let it catch up with you.

Why Retirement Rocks – Reason #97

Being retired means your friends and you can stop living at work and begin working at living.

Why Retirement Rocks – Reason #98

Retirement allows you the flexibility, in the words of Al Neuharth, to "Eat only when you are hungry. Drink only when you're thirsty. Sleep only when you're tired. Screw only when you're horny."

Why Retirement Rocks — Reason #99

"Travel is the frivolous part of serious lives, and the serious part of frivolous ones," stated Anne Sophie Swetchine. One of the best things about being retired is being able to travel when you want to travel — particularly when the cold of winter hits and you get to call your travel agent to have her send you away quickly to a much more warmer climate where there is certainly no snow.

Why Retirement Rocks — Reason #100

The hazards of workplace multi-tasking were mentioned earlier. In retirement multi-tasking takes on a completely new and interesting paradigm. For example, you can take a nap and water your plants at the same time, at your leisure, and without any negative consequences.

Why Retirement Rocks – Reason #101

No more memos from hell that knock you off your feet, saying you must take a pay decrease and work much longer hours because there is a serious recession going on. The purpose of all the other memos was to inflate mediocre ideas, obscure poor reasoning, and inhibit clarity.

Why Retirement Rocks – Reason #102

Greece no longer has to be just some place you see on the map of Europe. You actually get to visit it. Greece

is one of the most historically famous nations in the world. Known for its ancient civilization, incredible archaeological wonders, and several natural scenic attractions, Greece is a favorite destination for retirees. Located on the northwestern shores of the Mediterranean Sea, Greece is often cited as the cradle of Western Civilization. You may not only want to see the historical ruins of the Acropolis but also experience the Mediterranean beaches and its exotic nightlife and partying, especially at iconic Mykonos.

Why Retirement Rocks — Reason #103

When you first retired you thought that after a few months you would miss the challenges, the camaraderie, and the hustle and bustle of the workplace. In fact, you haven't missed any of these three one bit. Admit it; the only thing that you terribly miss now is not being able to call in sick at least two or three times a month.

Why Retirement Rocks — Reason #104

When you get really bored in retirement, you can get on the city bus. Ride it to the end of the line. Change buses. Repeat two times. This will still be more exciting than most of your former regular work activities used to be.

Why Retirement Rocks — Reason #105

When you are retired, you can define success on your own terms — and achieve it on your own terms. No more running after a carrot that the corporation enticed you into believing that you could catch — and which you or no other worker ever did.

Why Retirement Rocks — Reason #106

Whatever career you were in, you no longer have to face its occupational hazards. For example, for US  postal workers the cliché of dogs chasing mail carriers is no joke. More than 6,200 postal workers were attacked in 2017. Attacks on mail carriers climbed steadily since 2013, the *Washington Post* recently reported. The *Post* noted that the surge in bites coincided with the growth of home delivery of online purchases, exposing carriers more often to angry household pets.

Why Retirement Rocks – Reason #107

When the temptation arises, you can sleep in until mid-morning or noon and then proclaim to your friends, as W. Somerset Maugham once did, "It was such a beautiful morning I thought it would be a pity to get up."

Why Retirement Rocks – Reason #108

When you are working and 9 PM rolls around, it means it's time to go to bed. When you are retired, it means that your night is just starting.

Why Retirement Rocks – Reason #109

Retirement gives you the opportunity to utilize your best talents and your remarkable creativity on interesting projects that would never appear in most workplaces. For instance, you can produce your own pirate movie with you being the main star.

Why Retirement Rocks – Reason #110

Saturday no longer has to be a day when you are totally burnt out and incoherent due to your being so wound up during the previous five days of work.

Why Retirement Rocks — Reason #111

There will be many days when you think that retirement is one big-time cosmic joke. It is! So what? Work was even a bigger cosmic joke. Have a good laugh — compliments of the universe.

Why Retirement Rocks — Reason #112

You have more time to find joy in the finer things in life that working people don't, such as reading this silly book — and many other books. American writer and philosopher Ralph Waldo Emerson stated, "There is then creative reading as well as creative writing. When the mind is braced by labor and invention, the page of whatever book we read becomes luminous with manifold allusion. Every sentence is doubly significant, and the sense of our author is as broad as the world."

Why Retirement Rocks — Reason #113

You no longer have to deal with the constant confusion to which your company subjected you and your co-workers.

Why Retirement Rocks — Reason #114

Careers, money, and possessions are all okay in their little own ways. But, flat out — great friends provide much more satisfaction and happiness! Retirement allows you the time to spend a lot more time every day with friends. "To be rich in friends is to be poor in nothing," wrote American journalist Lilian Whiting.

Why Retirement Rocks — Reason #115

If you have always wanted to make a real difference in this world, retirement is the time to do it. You can begin by reading Nicole Bouchard Boles' book *How to Be an Everyday Philanthropist*, which shows you how to make the world a much better place without needing a large checkbook.

Why Retirement Rocks — Reason #116

Call it a corporate maze or a corporate prison. Retirement sets you free from whatever it is. English mathematician and scientist Isaac Newton concluded that "Truth is ever to be found in simplicity, and not in the multiplicity and confusion of things."

Why Retirement Rocks – Reason #117

In retirement, when you want to put more time in your life, you don't have to rush. You can slow down instead. In a magical way, the world will actually slow down for you.

Why Retirement Rocks – Reason #118

You no longer have to buy the expensive business suits that you wore to work. Instead, you can buy

several pairs of boots for all the various fun leisure activities in which you get to indulge. "Putting on fierce boots," proclaimed Nina Garcia, "is an instant pick-me-up." Not to be outdone, Daniel Berrigan said, "I'd like to die with my boots on."

Why Retirement Rocks — Reason #119

As many retirees finally get to do, you get to add "world traveler" to your bio. Lucius Annaeus Seneca (known simply as Seneca) was a Roman philosopher, dramatist, statesman, and one of the most eminent writers of the Silver Age of Latin literature. Even back in the first century AD during which he lived, he recognized the value of travel by pointing out that "Travel and change of place impart new vigor to the mind."

Why Retirement Rocks — Reason #120

Retirement provides you with more holistic abundance than you could ever receive by staying at your job and being untrue to yourself. There is incredible satisfaction in taking charge of your life at any age. Retirement is when you get to do this big time.

Why Retirement Rocks – Reason #121

As is to be expected, some people will have a big bug up their ass about your enjoying retirement life so much — but that's their problem. This will give you even more satisfaction knowing that you are doing the right thing with your life — and they are doing the wrong things with theirs.

Why Retirement Rocks – Reason #122

If you have developed some serious work related ailment, such as a back injury, sick building illness, repetitive stress injuries, or a constant migraine headache, retirement allows you the extra relaxation time required for using "belief-based healing." *National Geographic* in its December 2016 issue reported on the power of belief-based healing in an interesting article titled *Unlocking the Healing Power of You*. Retirement is the ideal time to heal yourself holistically because there is a lot less stress in your life than when you are working.

Why Retirement Rocks — Reason #123

Those fall mornings sure are pretty, aren't they? The brisk air and the smell of leaves no longer have to be short-lived because you have to hop the bus to go to work. You can now take full advantage of those fall mornings and fully appreciate them for all their worth.

Why Retirement Rocks — Reason #124

Nothing in the workplace is ever so bad that it can't be made a lot worse by firing the boss and hiring a new one. All things being equal, you will lose. All things being in your favor, you will still lose. What's more, win or lose, you will still lose big time. Indeed, there is no limit to how bad things can get. Trivial matters are usually handled promptly and the important matters are never solved. No matter how well you do your job, some superior will seek to modify the results. Teamwork is just another way to punish the high achievers like you for the pathetic mediocrity of the majority. The organization seems to have a much higher allotted number of positions to be filled with pathological misfits than even the most generous of spiritual gurus would ever tolerate. Viva la retirement!

Why Retirement Rocks – Reason #125

With the new found freedom that retirement brings, spontaneity can be exercised and experienced in its

truest sense. This means doing things at the spur of the moment, such as chopping a lot of wood, when impulse happens to strike. "People love chopping wood." observed Albert Einstein. "In this activity one immediately sees results."

Why Retirement Rocks – Reason #126

If your career was in the least ambitious of the sciences, that of twine and foil-collecting, for instance, retirement can actually increase your income because of the Social Security payments that you receive.

Why Retirement Rocks — Reason #127

Because you yourself don't have to go to work during summer and fall, you get to enjoy summer and fall days and no longer have to envy those individuals who are on their summer and fall vacations or are already themselves retired.

Why Retirement Rocks — Reason #128

No more having to go outside to wait for a bus to go to work when it's cold and raining is one of the benefits of being retired. You could catch pneumonia, run up a terrible hospital bill, linger a few weeks, and die a miserable death. Sure, this is a worst-case scenario, but it could happen.

Why Retirement Rocks – Reason #129

You no longer have to be a mere reflection of what others in the workplace sought you to be. Perhaps you were holding on to a facade, a life that wasn't meant for you. People at work left you no room to grow, to change, and to succeed in your own ways. Retirement allows you the opportunity to satisfy the urge to stay up all night to write or read or paint a picture from start to finish or practice playing the French horn until you are blue in the face.

Why Retirement Rocks – Reason #130

Your habit of procrastination can stop being "evil" once you retire. It can instead be a genius delight that you get to enjoy regularly, simply because most things in retirement can be put off until tomorrow or after tomorrow — without major consequences.

Why Retirement Rocks – Reason #131

On a whim, you can head out on a Las Vegas casino getaway, where you get to lose yourself in the mindless pursuit of blowing money on slot machines. However, do keep in mind these words of an unknown wise person: "People who can afford to gamble don't need money, and those who need money can't afford to gamble."

Why Retirement Rocks – Reason #132

No frantic last minute searches for appropriate office attire every morning. In retirement you can say, as Tom Masson said, "What if my trousers are shabby and worn, they cover a warm heart."

Why Retirement Rocks — Reason #133

If you were a middle manager before you retired, you no longer have to wonder, "Why does that lazy bunch of thieving bastard liars despise me so?"

Why Retirement Rocks — Reason #134

The alarm clock no longer has to be an instrument of constant restriction, limitation, and rude awakenings. It can now be relegated to a showpiece, a shadow of what it used to be.

Why Retirement Rocks – Reason #135

On those cold, winter mornings you can stay under the covers toasty warm until you feel like getting up, instead of freezing yourself silly waiting for a bus.

Why Retirement Rocks – Reason #136

If you have been killing time at work, waiting for life to shower you with meaning and happiness, this won't happen. Retirement will bring you meaning and happiness much more than work ever did if you learn how to establish your own purpose and structure in your life. Society's rules that you are supposed to live by are not sacred. Your own truths, principles, and agreements are, however.

Why Retirement Rocks — Reason #137

You can sit around and watch the sunset every night, regardless of what time the sun sets.

Why Retirement Rocks — Reason #138

Some unknown retiree claimed, "I used to have dreams that I died at my desk. Now that I have retired and am collecting Social Security, I don't have those

dreams anymore." The earlier you retire, the longer you get to collect your Social Security or other pension payments, taking as much money as you can out of the system. Those "heroes" who keep on working into their seventies, still paying into the system, thinking they are going to live to be ninety or a hundred, are the ones most likely to die on the job, collecting nothing.

Why Retirement Rocks – Reason #139

In retirement, having plenty of time during the day allows you to plan, prepare, and eat meals that you enjoy instead of stuffing down some unappetizing fast food before falling over from exhaustion at the end of a day at work.

Why Retirement Rocks – Reason #140

No more having to deal with a boss going off on irrelevant tangents when you ask him for a raise. Remember all the excuses that your boss gave you for not giving you a raise, the ones that were extremely vague and extremely complex with a puzzling air of mystery to them.

Why Retirement Rocks – Reason #141

If you were a tyrant of an executive at your last job, you no longer have to experience the veins in your forehead throbbing alarmingly as you enter the workplace, knowing full well that your subordinates hate your guts.

Why Retirement Rocks – Reason #142

You no longer have to ask yourself the following question: "If I really mess up at work at something that is going to cost the company $25,000, should I tell my boss?"

Why Retirement Rocks — Reason #143

Nasty rumors and corny gossip in the workplace are no longer a part of your life. Of course, all gossip isn't necessarily all bad. "Gossip can be quite entertaining," observed Vanna Bonta. "Occasionally, I've heard the most fascinating things about myself I never knew."

Why Retirement Rocks — Reason #144

You can lean back with your copy of *How to Retire Happy, Wild, and Free* and care not what happens. As the back cover of the book states, "Retirement is the beginning of life — not the end."

Why Retirement Rocks — Reason #145

You can practice the art of not finishing any or all projects that you undertake. That's right, no boss telling you to complete everything and on time. You can just drop the project and go on to something more interesting and exciting.

Why Retirement Rocks — Reason #146

If you were an engineering manager before you retired, you no longer have to spend all your time finding something wrong with every job your subordinate engineers did. Instead, in retirement you can find something wrong with everything you do.

Why Retirement Rocks — Reason #147

In the typical workplace most managers want to talk, few want to think, and none want to listen. What a relief to be retired and away from that moronic scene where all your suggestions were likely loudly laughed at or totally ignored in their entirety.

Why Retirement Rocks — Reason #148

Once you are retired, you get to party whenever you want, without having to fear losing a job if you get carried away and party for three straight days!

Why Retirement Rocks — Reason #149

If you have the book *1001 Places to See Before You Die*, being retired allows you much more opportunity to visit as many places listed in this great book as you would like to visit. It's hard to visit many places when you are working all year round except for a two or three week annual vacation.

Why Retirement Rocks — Reason #150

Alternatively, if you would like to restrict your travels to destinations solely in North America, being retired allows you the opportunity to visit as many places as possible listed in *1001 Places to See in the USA and Canada Before You Die*.

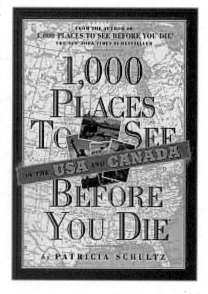

Why Retirement Rocks – Reason #151

You no longer have be part of a corporate culture where every major decision was always dumber than the last one.

Why Retirement Rocks – Reason #152

If you never felt the lure of the open sea as strongly as when you were in the workforce, retirement is when you finally get to satisfy this urge.

Why Retirement Rocks – Reason #153

Studs Terkel, a noted oral historian and radio broadcaster, in 1974 penned his classic book *Working* that investigates the meaning of work for different people under different circumstances. In a later book called *The Great Divide* Terkel cites American worker Isabelle Kuprin who talked about her job: "I'm a copywriter for an ad agency. It involves being a total asshole. I do it for the money, it's easy and horrible. I

do nothing good for society." If you feel the same way about your job as Isabelle Kruprin did about hers, the great news is that once you retire you don't have to be an asshole anymore. What's more, you won't have to read the book *Asshole No More* because being fully retired will help you to accomplish this gracefully.

Why Retirement Rocks – Reason #154

"The nail that sticks up gets hammered down," states a famous Japanese proverb. This particularly happens in most corporations. The great news is that once you retire you no longer have to be the one square peg trying to fit in a round hole.

Why Retirement Rocks — Reason #155

According to the British Dental Health Foundation, rising stress in the workplace is causing an increasing large number of professionals to grind their teeth while they sleep (and no doubt when they work). Bravo for retirement — which likely can cure grinding of teeth overnight.

Why Retirement Rocks — Reason #156

You can hang around pubs as much as you like. American Amanda Burger on her website (www.burgerabroad) talks about how she always looks forward to hanging out in British pubs. What makes them so special, as compared to bars all over the rest of the world, are the defining characteristics of a classic British Pub: 1. Classic décor. 2. Friendly patrons of the pub as well as all the staff. 3. Properly poured pints. 4. Real fires in stone fireplaces. 5. Dog friendly. In short, hanging out in a British pub is like hanging around in a friend's living room.

Why Retirement Rocks – Reason #157

Retirement means no more lazy, slipshod, careless, inept, cut-corner co-workers making fun of you by firing paper airplanes at you and calling you a "keener" just because you cared enough to do things right and wound up with the promotion and raise.

Why Retirement Rocks – Reason #158

You can forever perish the thought of having to work again in a corporate culture where its management proved that there is nothing too monstrous for humanity such as having employees jump through hoops just for the pleasure of seeing it done.

Why Retirement Rocks – Reason #159

A happy retirement doesn't care how hard you worked. Nor does it care whether you wear designer clothes. Nor does it care how fancy your car is. What's more, it clearly doesn't care how beautiful, talented, or intelligent you are. Retirement will teach you this important lesson: "It is what we value, not what we have, that makes us rich."

Why Retirement Rocks – Reason #160

You no longer have to be subjected to humorous and idiotic corporate policies and a moronic mission statement such as "Our mission is to deliver superior quality products for our customers through leadership, innovation, and partnerships", which was a lie and served no purpose other than to handsomely fatten the wallet of the rich management consultant brought in to help devise it using an uninformed focus group.

Why Retirement Rocks – Reason #161

You can hang out in New York as long as you want — one day, one week, or one month — for the sole great pleasure that hanging out in the city brings you. Use Google to find the 10 really cool things, 15 exciting things, 50 best things, 20 ultimate things, or 20 things to do alone in New York. The options are endless.

Why Retirement Rocks – Reason #162

No more having to think, "Nothing ahead but toil and drudgery for another fifty weeks," after your two short weeks of summer vacation are over.

Why Retirement Rocks — Reason #163

You can suspend forever the thought of having to get up in the morning, having to jump out of bed, and having to rush to get to work on time. You can now look forward to getting up each morning, knowing full well you can take your time to brew some fresh coffee and then continue on for the rest of the day at ease.

Why Retirement Rocks — Reason #164

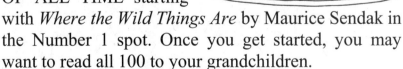

You have much more time to spend with your grandchildren and share the stories that were your favorites when you were a kid. Better still, on the Internet check out *Time* magazine's 100 BEST CHILDREN'S BOOKS OF ALL TIME starting with *Where the Wild Things Are* by Maurice Sendak in the Number 1 spot. Once you get started, you may want to read all 100 to your grandchildren.

Why Retirement Rocks – Reason #165

If you started your career at the bottom and stayed there all your working days, retirement can give you a new lease on life. You can hug yourself for making the great decision to retire and go on to greater heights from that point on.

Why Retirement Rocks – Reason #166

In retirement you no longer need a boss to tell you what to do and when to do it. Indeed, you get to find out that you are the best boss that you ever had. When you get blisters on your feet, you can order yourself to take a long rest, have the blisters heal a bit, and write a bit more of your book.

Why Retirement Rocks — Reason #167

You have the time to focus on an exercise regime and get your weight down to where it should be. Do remember these words from a health expert, however: "No exercise program will cure the harmful effects of a bad diet." Also, always keep in mind that it takes much longer to lose x number of pounds than to gain x number of pounds.

Why Retirement Rocks — Reason #168

No more of all your real talents being undervalued like they were at work. In retirement, you get to put your ingenuity, motivation, and the joy of life to good use on the projects that turn you on. As Jessica Hagy so rightfully pointed out, "It's more satisfying to dig a ditch with friends than to design a skyscraper with a team of sociopaths."

Why Retirement Rocks – Reason #169

With no job to dictate where you live, you can sell your house and move South or East or West or North — wherever houses are smaller and cheaper or where you truly want to live. *The Lazy Person's Guide to Happiness* advises, "Why waste so much time, energy, and trying to buy the biggest house that your credit rating will allow? Truth be known, a small house can hold as much happiness as a large one. Sometimes it will hold even more."

Why Retirement Rocks – Reason #170

On the other hand, if you really love the cozy shack where you live now, being retired means that you don't have to face the possibility of an employer demanding that you move to another state or country if you want to keep your job.

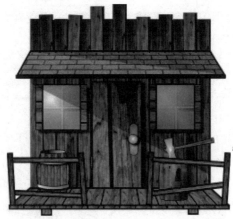

Why Retirement Rocks — Reason #171

Unlike the workplace, the coffee place where you hang out in your retirement offers you the opportunity to tell outrageously twisted jokes and have your peers appreciate them.

Why Retirement Rocks — Reason #172

If you were a manager in a financial institution before your retirement, the scandals of your administration no longer have to haunt you.

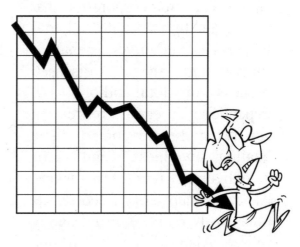

Why Retirement Rocks — Reason #173

In retirement your standards for success can happily be much lower than at work. You can quote Logan Pearsall Smith who cleverly proclaimed, "How can they say my life is not a success? Have I not for more than sixty years gotten enough to eat and escaped being eaten?"

Why Retirement Rocks — Reason #174

If you work in a corporation that is dysfunctional, with all co-workers' addictive behavior functioning in a diseased process of total idiotic co-dependency, early retirement can bring the freedom, holistic healing, wellness, and self-actualization that you desire. "The concept of freedom is never truly realized," said happy retiree Alan Major, "until one settles into retirement mode."

Why Retirement Rocks – Reason #175

You no longer have to experience a blow to your creative integrity by having your natural artistic talents manipulated by a corporation to produce some crude marketing ideas used in its misleading and unethical advertisements to sell products of dubious value.

Why Retirement Rocks – Reason #176

You can surf travel websites for last minute deals and pounce on irresistible cruise bargains to places like Mexico and the Caribbean, something that is not possible when you are working and have to give several months notice to take a vacation.

Why Retirement Rocks — Reason #177

No more being in a Dilbertized workplace where you have always been a puppet among many others hurdling toward failure. In retirement you can be a winner every day, thinking of many innovative ways to generate money from entrepreneurial projects. You may also want to think of innovative ways to spend the money. Indeed, you want to enjoy as much money as you can while you are alive and time it such that the last check that you write is to the undertaker — and it bounces!

Why Retirement Rocks — Reason #178

Retirement allows you the luxury to focus and get involved in the group of leisure activities that match your personality, skills, talents, and interests. For example, you can learn how to surf. Surfing is not a sport exclusive to the young and athletic. It's enjoyed by men

and women of all ages and can be learned in one's 50's and beyond. Surfing is an amazing workout and can enhance balance, coordination, and strengthen all parts of your body. Waikiki Beach in Honolulu is an excellent spot for the older beginner surfer with there being several surfing schools along the beach.

Why Retirement Rocks — Reason #179

No more having to learn the ropes of a difficult job. In fact, almost half of new hires say that "learning the ropes" is the most challenging part of starting a new job. Unfortunately, there's no legally-defined window when you are absolutely safe if your performance is not up to par. In the

U.S. you can be fired at any time for any legal reason, "even on your second day of work," business law attorney and employment law guru Beth Robinson told the website *Moneyish*.

Why Retirement Rocks — Reason #180

When you shop for groceries, not only can you choose to go at the time of day when the store is least busy, you can also choose to go the day that fresh produce has been stocked at the store.

Why Retirement Rocks – Reason #181

"The deepest personal defeat suffered by human beings," stated Ashley Montagu, "is constituted by the difference between what one was capable of becoming and what one has in fact become." If there is a big

difference between the type of individual you have become (because of where you worked) and the type of individual you would like to be, retirement certainly allows you the chance to correct this big mistake.

Why Retirement Rocks – Reason #182

In the workplace your words and actions are always in doubt. In retirement the wisdom of your words and actions speak for themselves.

Why Retirement Rocks – Reason #183

You can go to bed when you are tired — not at any particular hour at night or day.

Why Retirement Rocks – Reason #184

Because you are now free to move to another state such as California, you can finally stop getting speeding tickets in Washington State — and start getting speeding tickets in California.

Why Retirement Rocks — Reason #185

The day you retire is the day after which you don't ever have to wear a tie again. You will be much healthier for it. A July 2018 study published in the bona fide academic journal *Neuroradiology* found that wearing a tie can cut off the flow of blood to the brain by as much as 7.5 percent. The researchers referred to neckwear as "socially desirable strangulation." Even after the ties were loosened, the participants' cerebral blood flow continued to remain diminished by an average of 5.7 percent, according to an article in *Forbes*.

Why Retirement Rocks — Reason #186

On the other hand, if you are the type who likes wearing a tie — but only when you are barefoot — this is exactly what you get to do. Of course, there is no need to tighten your tie using the Windsor knot, for the classic look with a symmetrical, triangular knot. Because you are retired, you can wear a loose tie and not have the negative cerebrovascular effects that are associated with compressed jugular veins and carotids while wearing an overly tight necktie.

Why Retirement Rocks — Reason #187

You get to feel morally superior to working people because you have earned your retirement and they haven't. Indeed, you have wound up with Life's Golden Ticket for which you should be proud. While you are it, pay attention to this important advice from *Life's Secret Handbook*: "Relish life's small joys. It's all too easy to miss the small realizable pleasures in search of the elusive big ones."

Why Retirement Rocks — Reason #188

The fact that you are retired means that you never have to search for employment again. Without any doubt, searching for employment is one of the most demeaning tasks human beings have to face. As a gentleman named Ben commented in *Atlantic* magazine, "Worse [than looking for a job] is the demoralizing process that job searches have become . . . interviewers ask questions that reward liars and punish the truthful."

Why Retirement Rocks — Reason #189

In the modern world of full-time corporate work, your office is some stupid uncomfortable cubicle. In the modern world of doing gig work during your retirement or semi-retirement, your office is the golf course, the cabin in your yacht, or the most comfortable seat in a Starbucks coffee bar where you hang out with your laptop.

Why Retirement Rocks — Reason #190

For some people, the fear of flying on business trips is enough to leave them shaking like a leaf on a flight.

Estimates for prevalence have ranged between 2.5 percent and 6 percent. Research into the most effective ways to treat or manage fear of flying is difficult due to the inability to include a placebo in such studies. Therefore the best way to deal with the fear of flying is to be retired and not fly at all.

Why Retirement Rocks – Reason #191

After forty years of working in a career, not having to go to work is an incredible luxury — one that you have rightfully earned, however!

Why Retirement Rocks – Reason #192

The more cherished benefits of retirement by those who have retired early include:

- Every Monday feels like a holiday.
- Every Tuesday feels like a holiday.
- Every Wednesday feels like a holiday.
- Every Thursday feels like a holiday.
- Every Friday feels like a holiday.

Why Retirement Rocks — Reason #193

When you have burdens, errands, or obligations that appear urgent, you have the luxury of extra time to attend to them without panic.

Why Retirement Rocks — Reason #194

You can now live in a RV full time. For millions of Americans the RV lifestyle is their retirement dream, says Richard Parker, author of *Retire and Stay Retired: Enjoying the RV Lifestyle.* Traveling the highways and byways of America full time — who can ask for much more?

Why Retirement Rocks — Reason #195

When you were working and went on vacation, you took your laptop and cell phone to be connected to the workplace just in case something important came up. When you are retired and go on vacation, you can leave your cell phone and laptop at home so no one can find you.

Why Retirement Rocks — Reason #196

Perhaps you don't like screaming kids or kids in general, just dogs. As a retiree, when you want to visit your country's National parks, you have the choice to go before the beginning of June or after the end of August so that you can avoid vacationing families with kids out of school.

Why Retirement Rocks – Reason #197

You get to go to a lot more art show ceremonies and observe many more forms of art. Keep in mind the words of famous German author Johannes Wolfgang von Goethe who once remarked, "Individuality of expression is the beginning and end of all art."

Why Retirement Rocks – Reason #198

Retirement allows you to finally enjoy being yourself — the true you — not the false you who you were pretending to be when working in a career. Your idea of success can be your own. As Anna Quindlen said, "If your success is not on your own terms, if it looks good to the world but does not feel good in your heart, it is not success at all."

Why Retirement Rocks – Reason #199

After a weekend, you no longer have to face Mondays still in need of rest and recreation. Instead of hating Mondays, you can now love Mondays.

Why Retirement Rocks – Reason #200

Retirement allows you the time and opportunity to pursue old and new found dreams that you would never attain by keeping working eight or ten hours a day. As retiree and now published author (of four books) Robin Leigh Morgan recalled, "Becoming an author has been a dream I've had since I was a young child."

Why Retirement Rocks – Reason #201

With a job, on nice days you may skip work and then feel really guilty when you go golfing. In retirement, you just go golfing. No guilt at all!

Why Retirement Rocks – Reason #202

Many bosses are devious, solitary, secretive, and mean creatures. As the famous line in the song *Won't Get Fooled Again* by the British rock group The Who says, "Meet the new boss, same as the old boss." No more of this nonsense in retirement, thank God!

Why Retirement Rocks – Reason #203

Irrespective of your regret that you lost your youth a long time ago, perhaps you can do something about this. Spanish artist Pablo Picasso reminded us that, "Youth has no age." Retirement is a great time to reclaim your youth by any means that works for you. In short, as *Life's Secret Handbook* advises, you can forever be young in spirit.

Why Retirement Rocks – Reason #204

All your working life you have worked hard to afford the 3,000 square house that you purchased but never could sit back with a good book to enjoy. In retirement, you can do this every day of the week.

Why Retirement Rocks — Reason #205

In retirement if you don't know what day of the week it is — hey, no problem! You can just enjoy the day. The rest of the week will take care of itself. Understand that the success you have at any moment is the only real success you can ever experience. Reminisce about your great yesterdays, hope for many interesting tomorrows, but, above all, ensure that you live today.

Why Retirement Rocks — Reason #206

Every day feels like Saturday or Sunday — beer day, in other words. What's more, you can have a beer any time of the day, seven days a week. Syndicated humor columnist Dave Barry once declared, "Without any question, the greatest invention in the history of mankind is beer. Oh, I grant you that the wheel was also a fine invention, but the wheel does not go nearly as well with pizza."

Why Retirement Rocks – Reason #207

You get to weed the garden before the weeds get out of control. Keep in mind, however, "A good garden may have some weeds," according to Thomas Fuller. Moreover, as A. A. Milne once observed, "Weeds are flowers too, once you get to know them."

Why Retirement Rocks – Reason #208

If you worked at a government agency or a corporation with a good pension plan, you can collect a pension from your primary career and earn more money from a side gig in retirement doing something that you truly enjoy doing.

Why Retirement Rocks — Reason #209

If deep down there has always been something that appealed to you about the cool Starbucks laptop-and-cappuccino crowd, you can now be part of it. Indeed, you can become a digital nomad, making money on your laptop part time, being semi-retired. Your office can be the Starbucks where your laptop and you happen to be at any time.

Why Retirement Rocks — Reason #210

You can go back to college and have much more fun than the first time around. What's more, you can get a degree in some discipline for the fun of it instead of for the purpose of getting a job. Here's the biggest advantage of going back to school as a retiree: If you cut classes, no one calls your parents.

Why Retirement Rocks – Reason #211

No more crying at 3 PM each workday afternoon like you used to do in the workplace because it was still two hours away from quitting time. If you were like me when I was working as an Engineer for five and a half years, the best time of your working day was quitting time. Of course, the second best time of the working day was lunch time.

Why Retirement Rocks – Reason #212

One of life's great pleasures is getting the pension check in the mail. Indeed, you get to live *The Retiree's Creed*:

Early to bed;
Sleep in late.
Collect your pension;
Ain't life great!

Why Retirement Rocks — Reason #213

Because you will likely spend more time at home when you retire, you have a better chance of catching your cat in the act of doing something evil. But there again, as famous Spanish writer Miguel de Cervantes commented, "Those who'll play with cats must expect to be scratched."

Why Retirement Rocks — Reason #214

You get to try many different leisure activities and get to find out that some — such as ice fishing — are not for everyone.

Why Retirement Rocks – Reason #215

You can wear as many hats as you want to wear once you retire. Try this when you are working and see what happens!

Why Retirement Rocks – Reason #216

Being retired means that you no longer have to be overly stressed while catching work-related flights. The fatigue and logistics of getting to another city to lead a training seminar or attend a networking event are things that you can certainly do without.

Why Retirement Rocks — Reason #217

No more frayed nerves from having to commute to work every workday in your car on the freeway where traffic is always slow and heavy.

Why Retirement Rocks — Reason #218

Indeed, commuting to work and back is never fun. Commuting can rob you of a major part of your life. In 2016 Canadian commuters spent an average of 26.2 minutes traveling to their workplace and another 26.2 minutes back home. Worse, workers in London, England endure an 81-minute commute, equivalent to 38 working days a year. Nearly 3.7 million of Londoners spend two hours a day commuting. With the dejection of your having to commute to work being a distant memory, you can drive only when it is pleasurable to do so.

Why Retirement Rocks – Reason #219

Statistics indicate that you will likely live to eighty-five. You may die a lot younger than you expect, however. By retiring early, you at least get to collect a few pension checks instead of none.

Why Retirement Rocks – Reason #220

The first sign of snow does not have be a sad event because as a snowbird retiree you know that you will soon be heading out to Florida or Mexico or Hawaii for six months.

Why Retirement Rocks — Reason #221

As a retiree, you now have the time and energy to do the dishes right after dinner each night unlike when you were in the workforce. Then you used to have the dishes pile for days before you did them.

Why Retirement Rocks — Reason #222

Retirement means no more cubicles! A study cited in *Harvard Business Review* concluded that workers in enclosed offices were by far the happiest, reporting the least amount of frustration on all 15 of the factors surveyed. Workers in cubicles with high partitions were the most miserable, reporting the lowest rates of satisfaction in 13 out of those 15 factors.

Why Retirement Rocks — Reason #223

No more experiencing depression on Sunday evenings because you have to go to work on Monday mornings but are still suffering from carpel tunnel injuries from Fridays' repetitive wrist work.

Why Retirement Rocks — Reason #224

You have a lot more time to get to know your neighbors and to spend time with them.

Why Retirement Rocks – Reason #225

At home your air conditioner always worked properly. In the workplace the only time the air conditioner worked was in winter and never in summer. Even so, you stuck to your belief in the work ethic and continued to suffer until your retirement. Being retired gave you time to reflect about the nature of hard work and the work ethic itself. Today these words by English novelist and poet D. H. Lawrence resonate with you big time: "You'll never succeed in idealizing hard work. Before you can dig mother earth you've got to take off your ideal jacket. The harder a man works at brute labor, the thinner becomes his idealism, the darker his mind."

Why Retirement Rocks – Reason #226

No more being in the high tension workplace and being so forgetful that you forget what you were trying to remember.

Why Retirement Rocks – Reason #227

During your working years all your neighbor always had a nicer lawn than you did. Now that you are retired, you have time to create the nicest lawn on the block and make all of your working neighbors "green" with envy.

Why Retirement Rocks – Reason #228

With all the extra time that you have to play and exercise with your dog, your dog nor you has to ever get out of shape again.

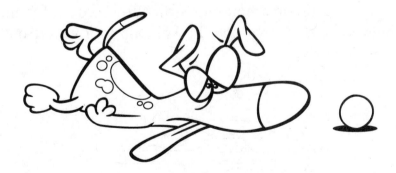

Why Retirement Rocks – Reason #229

No more having to dream up of creative and not-so-creative ways to kill workplace boredom.

Why Retirement Rocks – Reason #230

Your spouse's and your dream of living on a house boat can finally be a reality. You can achieve a sense of satisfaction that living in an ordinary house just doesn't provide. No lawn or yard work or snow to shovel. No property taxes to pay. No commute and no automobile traffic to hassle with. You can have a constant view of the water that won't be blocked by someone building a house or structure in front of your home. Best of all, you get to wake up to a waterfront view every day.

Why Retirement Rocks – Reason #231

Retirement gives you the opportunity to plant at least one tree in your life. In fact, with all the time you have, you may want to plant many. French philosopher Voltaire whose works epitomize the Age of Enlightenment stated,

"The planting of a tree is a modest form of immortality and one of the few truly long-term expressions of hope to mortal human beings." Russell Page claimed that, "To plant trees is to give body and life to one's dreams of a better world." Still more, billionaire Warren Buffett pointed out that "Someone's sitting in the shade today because someone planted a tree a long time ago."

Why Retirement Rocks – Reason #232

No more silly efforts like when you were in the workplace, trying to work on your laptop while on the run. Retirement convinced you that this was a case of lost labor. "Yet it is in our idleness, in our dreams," remarked Virginia Woolf, "that the submerged truth sometimes comes to the top."

Why Retirement Rocks – Reason #233

You can stop in the middle of whatever you are doing and go out to eat, if you wish! Going to eat by yourself is not only for single people, by the way. As comedian Henny Youngman once quipped, "Some people ask the secret of our long marriage. We take time to go to a restaurant two  times a week. A little candlelight, dinner, soft music and dancing. She goes Tuesdays, I go Fridays."

Why Retirement Rocks – Reason #234

Retirement gives you the opportunity to be yourself. It always seems easier to live the comfortable and the conventional, to fit in with the majority. It's when you live the uncomfortable and unconventional, however, that you make the most of your best talents, your creativity, and your own actions. That is also when your life starts being fun, satisfying, and meaningful.

Why Retirement Rocks — Reason #235

H. L. Mencken, an American editor and critic of the complacent American middle class, stated, "The only liberty an inferior man really cherishes is the liberty to quit work, stretch out in the sun, and scratch himself." Retirement gives you the right to exercise this liberty.

Why Retirement Rocks — Reason #236

You have sufficient time to read all of the morning newspaper and don't have to wait until after work to finish it. An unknown happy retiree remarked, "Retirement is the time in your life when time is no longer money."

Why Retirement Rocks — Reason #237

Number 5 on the list of the workplace's most annoying habits is an uncaring co-worker who consistently hums or whistles. Being retired means that you no longer have to put up with that office jerk humming the theme songs from Bonanza and Pink Panther all day.

Why Retirement Rocks — Reason #238

You don't have to miss the fall experience due to your being confined to an office during the day.

Why Retirement Rocks – Reason #239

No more being intimidated into paying for co-workers' birthday gifts. The worst case was when the boss having the birthday collected money for his own birthday gift.

Why Retirement Rocks – Reason #240

You get to enjoy the finer things in life a little more often because you have the time for them. The finer things in life can include a favorite piece of chocolate, a sauna, champagne breakfasts, a pair of Doc Martins, dining out at a fine restaurant, and reading an inspiring book on a cool and rainy afternoon.

Why Retirement Rocks – Reason #241

Taking early retirement means that you no longer have to face the danger of blowing your blood vessels due  to the stress at work and winding up in the hospital for days. Indeed, you want to save your health for your retirement. Today's retirees, according to numerous surveys, say in no uncertain terms that the number-one ingredient for a happy retirement is, by no small margin, having your health.

Why Retirement Rocks – Reason #242

No need to hire expensive and over-priced contractors to put a new roof on your house. Being retired means that you have the time to do this yourself and do a much better job than the slipshod contractors would do. This in itself will give  you a sense of satisfaction and accomplishment that most of your work activities never gave you.

Why Retirement Rocks — Reason #243

Poet e. e. cummings warned us that "To be yourself in a world that is doing its best, day and night to make you like everybody else — is to fight the hardest battle any human being can fight; and never stop fighting." Of course, this battle is much easier won when one is retired than when one is working in a corporation or in government.

Why Retirement Rocks — Reason #244

As you happily fly your antique airplane across America, you get the opportunity to explode the myth — forever — that retirement is tough on everyone!

Why Retirement Rocks – Reason #245

In your retirement years your needs change for the better. Retiree M. Mushol who was featured in a PBS documentary about retirement boasted, "We have no porch, no rocking chair — and no time. My biggest need is a calendar because there are so many things to do. Now I encourage people to retire — the younger the better."

Why Retirement Rocks – Reason #246

When you are retired, and it's not a beautiful morning, it is easy to have your cheerfulness make it one. When you have to go into a toxic workplace, this is much more difficult to accomplish.

Why Retirement Rocks – Reason #247

When you retire, you finally get to switch to a new boss — from the one who hired you to the one who married you.

Why Retirement Rocks – Reason #248

You no longer have to have thoughts such as, "No doubt the strain of this totally dysfunctional workplace will crack me sooner or later."

Why Retirement Rocks – Reason #249

The failure — total seizure, in fact — of your imagination that was so prevalent in the workplace for so many years can now be put to rest and replaced with mental playfulness, natural curiosity, and eagerness to learn.

Why Retirement Rocks – Reason #250

American writer Joseph Heller stated, "I think that in every company today there is always at least one person who is going crazy slowly." Once you retire, you don't have to be that person any more.

Why Retirement Rocks – Reason #251

You can watch sports events as they happen — regardless of what time of the day — instead of watching replays, when the event is long over, and you already know the score or results.

Why Retirement Rocks – Reason #252

You can also watch horror movies until dawn, without having to think about going to work in the morning.

Why Retirement Rocks – Reason #253

You no longer have to be part of a corporate culture that in more ways than one raised stupidity to the status of a religion. As Martin Luther King, Jr. stated, "Nothing in the world is more dangerous than sincere ignorance and conscientious stupidity."

Why Retirement Rocks – Reason #254

You get to treat yourself big time with a lot of gifts for having made such a great decision — to retire early and live life the way it was supposed to be lived. These retirement gifts include:

- The gift of laughter
- The gift of freedom
- The gift of not having to go to work
- The gift of great health
- The gift of great friends
- The gift of a good night's sleep every night of the week

Why Retirement Rocks — Reason #255

No more having to work late into the night on corporate projects that have deadlines and cause you many sleepless nights.

Why Retirement Rocks — Reason #256

On the other hand, being retired means that you get to feel on top of the world as you work late into the night on your hobby website or blog, especially when it earns you much more money than you ever made in your career.

Why Retirement Rocks — Reason #257

In retirement you can finally get rid of some of your workplace baggage. For example, you no longer have to vicariously live through your corporation hoping that its accomplishments will eventually be recognized

on a global scale, validate your wasted career, and in some way compensate you for all the opportunities that you missed by not striking it on your own to really make a difference in this world.

Why Retirement Rocks — Reason #258

Retirement allows you to live so that when your grandchildren think of fairness, caring, and integrity, they immediately think of you. When you were in the workplace, it was difficult to cultivate these traits.

Why Retirement Rocks – Reason #259

Regardless of the time of the week that a friend has to move, you can be available to help. As the old joke goes, "A good friend will help you move and a really good friend will help you move a body."

Why Retirement Rocks – Reason #260

You get to joyfully talk to your friends on the phone for hours at a time — something you were not able to do when you were in the workforce. You can do Oscar Wilde proud who quipped, "Conversation should touch everything but should concentrate itself on nothing."

Why Retirement Rocks — Reason #261

You have much more time to strengthen your bonds with those you love.

Why Retirement Rocks — Reason #262

No more looney co-workers driving you bonkers with their mean workplace pranks. In this case, it was particularly disturbing given that you forgot to bring your umbrella that day.

Why Retirement Rocks – Reason #263

You can join Toastmasters, something that you did not have time for when in the work world and become a master at making inspirational and motivational speeches. Do charge for your services when you start making speeches to professional groups. As Mark Twain said, "He charged nothing for his preaching – and it was worth it too."

Why Retirement Rocks – Reason #264

No more having to meet with a boss. The workplace is full of bosses who are incompetent and don't realize that they are. This is to be found in the work of professors Justin Kruger and David Dunning and has become well known as the Dunning-Kruger effect. Incompetent people often suffer from delusions of superiority that result in their vastly overrating their own abilities. Worse, they tend to not recognize the higher skill level in others. Worst of all, because they do not recognize their lack of skills, these bosses never adopt new ones or change their unproductive behavior.

Why Retirement Rocks – Reason #265

You can get finally get a fun retirement job, something you wanted to do as a kid — such as driving an eighteen-wheeler cross country — and work for the fun of it instead of for the money.

Why Retirement Rocks – Reason #266

You get to truly relax with every cup of coffee — and enjoy coffee the way it was meant to be enjoyed. Coffee needs to taste good and needs to taste good 365 days a year. Having an espresso or cappuccino two or three times a day should not be done as a special occasion but as a way of retirement life.

Why Retirement Rocks – Reason #267

If you were the main bread winner when you were working fulltime, you no longer have to be motivated every work day by your wife to get out of bed and go to work so you won't be fired. Being retired means that you can stay toasty warm in bed and get up when you are ready to get up. Of course, your wife also doesn't have to get out of bed early.

Why Retirement Rocks – Reason #268

Decision making is easy. Being retired means you can make decisions by flipping a coin — simply because choice A will likely be just as much fun as choice B.

Why Retirement Rocks – Reason #269

"Great spirits have always encountered violent opposition from mediocre minds," observed Albert Einstein. In your working life, having a great idea means that practically everyone at the workplace is going to violently suppress it for one reason or another. In retirement, having a great idea means putting it to good use for your best personal gain. British philosopher and economist John Stuart Mill added to this so well when he said, "The great creative individual . . . is capable of more wisdom and virtue than collective man ever can be."

Why Retirement Rocks – Reason #270

You finally can buy a Harley and join a raunchy biker's club, bragging about this on Facebook — without having to fear being found out by your company and being fired for improper conduct.

Why Retirement Rocks — Reason #271

No more embarrassing work-related injuries that you used to get while employed as a tradesperson — particularly when you worked with a so-called "team."

Why Retirement Rocks — Reason #272

You have the time and opportunity to look up that weird classmate from college who you haven't seen in thirty-five years.

Why Retirement Rocks – Reason #273

Hardly anyone likes or enjoys their commute in whatever form it takes. Taking the London Tube in summer during rush hour is tough but it's particularly hellish when there are delays, such as in August 2017 when commuters were stuck underground for over an hour during the morning rush hour after a major power failure crippled three Tube lines. To be sure, not having to commute to work on the underground line where you have to stand most of the time is one of the greatest benefits of retirement.

Why Retirement Rocks – Reason #274

"Gainfully unemployed, very proud of it, too," wrote Charles Baxter in *The Feast of Love*. You can be that proud, gainfully unemployed individual in your retirement. Even doing laundry is a pleasure because you get to do it leisurely, with swagger, and when you feel like it.

Why Retirement Rocks – Reason #275

If you felt that school was a waste of twelve years of your life that you will never get back (as famous singer Ry Cooder felt), and that work was another waste of forty years of your life that you will never get back, ten years of retirement done right will make up for it. You can move to Panama like my ex-Toronto friend Liz did and live in a condo by the beach. For her, every day is beach day.

Why Retirement Rocks – Reason #276

In the workplace you were always scared that your boss would yell at you. From your first retirement day onward you no longer have to spend most of your week days hiding from your boss in situations such as under your desk, in a bathroom stall, in the meeting room, or wearing a disguise.

Why Retirement Rocks – Reason #277

You get to meet new friends who will introduce you to new leisure activities such as playing horseshoes. New friends and new leisure activities are great ways to enhance your enjoyment of life.

Why Retirement Rocks – Reason #278

You no longer have the feeling that your work is not useful to society. Instead you get to feel that your leisure pursuits are truly useful to you.

Why Retirement Rocks — Reason #279

Another advantage of being retired is having the extra time to help your children. As retiree Helen Rich once said, "When my son and daughter-in-law asked me to stay at their house for a week to house-sit while they were away on vacation, I had the freedom to do it."

Why Retirement Rocks — Reason #280

When extreme bad weather conditions strike, such as hurricanes or tornados, you no longer have to decide whether to venture outside to go to work.

Why Retirement Rocks — Reason #281

In the workplace, there are days when it takes all you have got just to keep up with the losers. Once you retire, you no longer have any of these days.

Why Retirement Rocks — Reason #282

As a retiree, unlike when you were a worker, you can go for coffee or lunch and not have to go back to the office to face a mountain of work that wasn't there when you left.

Why Retirement Rocks – Reason #283

Retirement may help you to stop cheating on your spouse. An Australian 2018 survey says that one's profession is an indicator of whether a person is likely to cheat. According to Victoria Milan, an affair dating website, people working in finance are most likely to stray and cheat on their partners. This includes bankers, brokers, and analysts. The profession ringing in at second most likely to cheat were those in the airline industry, mainly pilots and flight attendants. Healthcare professionals, business owners, and sports pros rounded out the top five. Apparently many people cheat because of the extreme stress of their jobs. Of course, this factor is no longer valid in retirement.

Why Retirement Rocks – Reason #284

Do you remember the song "If you want to get to Heaven, you have to raise a little Hell" by the Ozark Mountain Dare Devils? On that note, retirement affords you much more time and freedom to raise a little Hell so that you increase your chances of getting to Heaven.

Why Retirement Rocks — Reason #285

You get to call a two-hour lunch break "a short lunch break" in retirement because a normal lunch break in retirement is normally three hours.

Why Retirement Rocks — Reason #286

You have total freedom insofar as dressing up to match the occasion. Formal dress for you in retirement can mean wearing old shoes with untied shoelaces.

Why Retirement Rocks — Reason #287

Retirement allows you to, as the Chinese proverb advises, "Always take an emergency leisurely."

Why Retirement Rocks — Reason #288

The Sufi poet Jalaluddin Rumi once wrote that even Jesus fled from the fool, saying, "I can make the blind see, the deaf hear, the lame run and raise the dead, but I cannot turn the fool away from his folly." That being the case, it's wise to flee any workplace that has a lot of fools working there, particularly those who are indecisive whiners, incompetent bimbos, and lazy goof-offs. Retirement is the ideal way of doing this.

Why Retirement Rocks – Reason #289

Where you live doesn't have to be dictated by your job. Indeed, you can become a global nomad with no  home and no fixed address. In this regard, retirement gives you the opportunity to shake up your life, to seek adventure outside your comfort zone, and to fiercely focus on experiences instead of material things.

Why Retirement Rocks – Reason #290

Zappa's Law states, "There are two things on earth that are universal: hydrogen and stupidity." This is also true in the typical workplace — except the hydrogen may be in short supply. It's better to retire early than to continue to be angry about the universal corporate stupidity and have to deal with it every day.

Why Retirement Rocks – Reason #291

In a November 2016 *Forbes* article about the top-10 reasons why people hate their jobs, the number 3 reason was: "Their employer disregards their personal life and has no compassion for their obligations

outside of work." From your retirement day onward you don't have to receive cell calls from your boss on weekends demanding that you come into work for so-called emergencies. Plain and simple, that bastard-rat-of-a-boss was a sadist who wanted to make you suffer in any way possible.

Why Retirement Rocks – Reason #292

No more having to listen to your boss's plot about how he intends to help you improve your character.

Why Retirement Rocks — Reason #293

By leaving the workplace for good, you get to prove that the work ethic was a terrible mistake — a cute term gone haywire! If work was so wonderful, the rich, famous, and powerful of the corporate world would have saved all of it for themselves.

Why Retirement Rocks — Reason #294

Life's Secret Handbook states, "Death often comes at a bad time." By retiring early, you don't have to tempt fate and die working. British writer W. Somerset Maugham's last words reportedly were, "Dying is a very dull, dreary affair. My advice to you is to have nothing whatever to do with it." Sure, you can't avoid dying — but you may be able to put it off for many years if you retire early.

Why Retirement Rocks — Reason #295

With all the extra time you have for friendship in retirement, you get to find out that although money might make you wealthy, friends make you rich.

Why Retirement Rocks — Reason #296

You also get to find out as Horace Walpole pointed out: "Old friends are the great blessing of one's later years . . . They have a memory of the same events and have the same mode of thinking."

Why Retirement Rocks – Reason #297

Still more about friendship: You get to find out that there is no physician in your retirement years as good as a true friend.

Why Retirement Rocks – Reason #298

No more having to hire a gardener to trim the hedges and mow the lawn like you used to have to do when you were working and too busy to do it yourself. Now the job gets done on time and the way you would like it done.

Why Retirement Rocks — Reason #299

You now can take many creative liberties with your life as opposed to the time when you were working.

Why Retirement Rocks — Reason #300

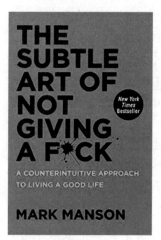

In working life you get to read the great advice in *The Subtle Art of Not Giving a F*ck* and put it to good use — but you have to be subtle about it. In retirement life you don't have to be subtle about it at all. You just plainly don't give a f*ck! Heck, you don't even have to read the book.

Why Retirement Rocks — Reason #301

You can become the expert on how to retire happy, wild, and free — particularly the "wild" part. Do let us know how it all turns out, okay!

Why Retirement Rocks — Reason #302

Retirement gives you the opportunity to live your life with much more excitement. The cult novel *The Dice Man* explores what would happen if you decided to surrender your personality and free will to the random roll of a dice. In the book, the main character uses the dice to make decisions. He ends up conducting extramarital affairs, sabotaging his career, and ultimately founds a cult by giving his every step in life six options and slavishly obeying whichever the dice chooses for him. Sam Parker of *Huffington Post UK* tried this in real life. One weekend he was a busker, an artist, and a beard fetishist by day and by night, both the life and soul of a party, and its dullest guest. Parker concluded "that there are a lot of benefits [and drawbacks] of this utterly irresponsible, gloriously anarchic, and weirdly addictive approach to life."

Why Retirement Rocks – Reason #303

Whatever you are doing in retirement, when you get tired, you can just rest and experience the tiredness until it goes away. Try this in the workplace and see how long you keep your job.

Why Retirement Rocks – Reason #304

What a relief it is not to have a boss looking over your shoulder trying to figure out what you are doing and making sure that you are working on something he deems important. Just as annoying was the employee who was the "office hoverer." He stopped by to ask an irrelevant or stupid question and then stuck around for no reason, making small talk. The office hoverer was also known to look over your shoulder as you worked.

Why Retirement Rocks — Reason #305

No more being overanalyzed by every personality-based algorithm known to Facebook founder Mark Zuckerberg. From your retirement day onward you don't have to take the latest trendy corporate on-line training program, such as the dicey one on emotional intelligence, which did you absolutely no good. Neither did the expensive anger management course do you any good, particularly when your corporation asked you to pay for all of its cost out of your own pocket.

Why Retirement Rocks — Reason #306

In your work life past you felt obligated to go to a company Christmas or New Years Eve party and then ended up making a fool of yourself. It's a lot more fun to be retired and to go to parties where you can make a fool of yourself and there are no major consequences.

Why Retirement Rocks – Reason #307

Munder's Law in the *Murphy's Law* book states that everyone who doesn't work has a scheme that does. Retirement from the typical workplace is a great time to put your questionable scheme that requires little or no work to profitable use.

Why Retirement Rocks – Reason #308

You will have reached the pinnacle of success when you don't have to be competitive for the company's sake, which just chained you to your job for many years. In their song *Already Gone*, the American rock band The Eagles sang, "So often times it happens that we live our lives in chains. And we never even know we have the key." For those who can afford it, the key is to retire.

Why Retirement Rocks – Reason #309

Let's face it. As a genius, no matter how well you perform your job, a superior will seek to modify the results. Another pitfall of being a genius is that overbearing bosses don't want an employee who is smarter than them all the time. Louis Aragon said it so well: "We know that the nature of genius is to provide idiots with ideas twenty years later." No question, you can show your genius qualities best when you retire.

Why Retirement Rocks – Reason #310

In the workplace, you are forced to work for years with blokes who you can't stand. In retirement, if you meet a new person who is not a good match for your personality, you walk away for good.

Why Retirement Rocks — Reason #311

As soon as you retire you can live by this wonderful motto: "Didn't care yesterday. Didn't care today. Probably won't care tomorrow either."

Why Retirement Rocks — Reason #312

You can't help but feel superior to the mass of corporate humanity because you know with certainty that you don't need a corporation to spoon feed you with a job and take care of you with its sponsored health care plan anymore.

Why Retirement Rocks – Reason #313

No more going to a corporate office on Monday morning and hearing co-workers ask each other that mundane question "How was your weekend?" followed by answers such as "It was fine." Fact is, you never did care whether any of your boring co-workers enjoyed their weekends, did you?

Why Retirement Rocks – Reason #314

You can spend a lot more time alone. In solitude a lot of us can feel less alone than we felt in the workplace. "I never found the companion that was so companionable as solitude," said Henry David Thoreau. "Conversation enriches the understanding, but solitude is the school of genius,"

advised Edward Gibbon. Still more, Dr. Wayne Dyer reminded us that "You cannot be lonely if you like the person you're alone with."

Why Retirement Rocks – Reason #315

You no longer have to drive your car as if your journey is the only one on Earth that is going to save the entire Universe.

In retirement life you have more time to relax and realize that your journey is rather insignificant in the higher order of the Universe.

Why Retirement Rocks – Reason #316

To be sure, dealing with nasty neighbors can be enough to drive even the most peaceful person to the brink. If you have terrible neighbors, you can sell your house once you retire and buy a R.V. (Heaven on Four Wheels) with the proceeds. If the neighborhood that you are parked in is way too noisy, you can head out any time you want and find a much better neighborhood in which to hang out.

Why Retirement Rocks — Reason #317

You can have your retirement dream come true — living in a little cabin somewhere by the sea. As American actress Christina Applegate remarked, "My dream is to have a house on the beach, even just a little shack somewhere so I can wake up, have coffee, look at dolphins, be quiet, and breathe the air."

Why Retirement Rocks — Reason #318

It has been said that company cafeteria food can kill you. By having retired early and having avoided more cafeteria food, you have increased your life expectancy by about 27 years. Putting things in the best possible way, Denis Diderot told us, "Doctors are always working to preserve our health and cooks to destroy it, but the latter are the more often successful."

Why Retirement Rocks — Reason #319

In the same vein, having to take a bag lunch to work (in order to save money or because your lunch hour wasn't long enough to take an off-site lunch) seldom translated into a gourmet's delight. Those sardine sandwiches didn't taste all that good — particularly when it was the fifth day in the row that you had to eat them! Furthermore, when you brought a gourmet lunch, chances were that some lunch-stealing co-worker would eat it.

Why Retirement Rocks — Reason #320

You can indulge in all the alluring bird and butterfly watching you have been meaning to do — and the birds and the butterflies can enjoy watching you even more. Do let us know if you ever see a blue butterfly since it has spiritual significance in a diverse group of religious disciplines that includes, interestingly, Christianity.

Why Retirement Rocks — Reason #321

In a turbulent world, we all crave ways to organize, classify, and tidy up. In retirement, you finally have the time to organize your bedroom closet — and even more time to keep it organized!

Why Retirement Rocks — Reason #322

No more having to get up at 6 AM on weekdays to go to work. What a drag that used to be. It was bad for

your health, too! A recent study by researchers from University of Pittsburgh found that routine (and at first sight harmless) sleep changes, such as waking up very early to go to the workplace, can increase the risk for diabetes and heart disease.

Why Retirement Rocks — Reason #323

In retirement, eating on the run is no longer part of your lifestyle as it was when you were working. Carl Honoré, in his book *In Praise of Slowness*, cautioned, "In our fast-forward culture, we have lost the art of eating well. Food is often little more than fuel to pour down the hatch while doing other stuff — surfing the Web, driving, walking along the street. Dining al desko is now the norm in many workplaces. All of this speed takes a toll. Obesity, eating disorders, and poor nutrition are rife."

Why Retirement Rocks — Reason #324

If you like sipping elegant red wine, such as the full-bodied Australian Mollydooker The Boxer Shiraz or the full-bodied Spanish Tridente Tempranillo, you get to use this saying with your friends more often: "Wine gets better with age, and the older I get, the more I like it." While drinking the wine, keep in mind these fine words of Carl Honoré: "It is stupid to drink a glass of wine quickly. And it is stupid to play Mozart too fast."

Why Retirement Rocks — Reason #325

If you have never done this before, you can finally find the time to learn how to swim for better or worse. Lieutenant-General Robert Baden-Powell, founder of The Boy Scouts and founder of the Girl Guides, stated, "Swimming has its educational value — mental, moral, and physical — in giving you a sense of mastery over an element, and of power of saving life, and in the development of wind and limb."

Why Retirement Rocks — Reason #326

You get to be extremely leisurely and carefree — regardless of the task you undertake.

Why Retirement Rocks – Reason #327

The crazy hedonism that you enjoyed only on weekends when you were working can now be enjoyed every day of the week. What's more, you get to prove, as Laurence J. Peter stated, "The time you enjoy wasting is not wasted time." Indeed, retirement is like being out of school for the summer but the summer never ends.

Why Retirement Rocks – Reason #328

To your friends still in the workforce you can say, "You know that Social Security deduction they keep taking out of your paycheck? Well, it's happily helping pay for my retirement, but sadly financial advisors say there may be nothing left in the rapidly diminishing Social Security fund for you when you decide to retire."

Why Retirement Rocks – Reason #329

You can now climb that one mountain that you wanted to climb in your lifetime. As *Life's Secret Handbook* states, "You can climb Mount Everest 'because it's there.' Or you can climb an imaginary mountain 'because it isn't there.' Which do you think will bring you more satisfaction and happiness?"

Why Retirement Rocks – Reason #330

You can do 100 things that you have never thought of doing — such as "drive cross-country with Richard Simmons." That was one of the "Top 10 Things to Do in Retirement" (#3) that David Letterman came up with. If you try this, let us know how this one all turns out, okay!

Why Retirement Rocks – Reason #331

No more meetings. No more commuting. No more cubicles. No more boss. You get to win the "Not Working and Loving It" award.

Why Retirement Rocks – Reason #332

You can say goodbye to feeling so burnt out from work on Wednesday morning, wondering how you are going to make in through the day, let alone the rest of the week and the weekend.

Why Retirement Rocks – Reason #333

If you are a baseball fan, you can go to all the afternoon games that your home team plays instead of  having to miss games because you have to be at work. If you aren't a baseball fan, perhaps you should become one. U.S. scholar Jacques Barzun once claimed, "Whoever wants to know the heart and mind of America had better learn baseball, the rules and realities of the game."

Why Retirement Rocks – Reason #334

Life seems to go by so quickly. We are so busy watching out for what is ahead of us that we don't have time to enjoy where we are. Life becomes a blur. Often it takes some calamity to make us live in the present. That or retirement.

Why Retirement Rocks – Reason #335

Long-term job strain is worse for your heart than gaining forty pounds in weight or aging thirty years, according to a 2003 US study. It follows that by retiring early from an extremely stressful job you can improve your health dramatically and afford to eat an extra cheeseburger or two every week.

Why Retirement Rocks – Reason #336

Retirement is the time to put to use all the information from the world's best retirement books. Google "best retirement books" to find out which ones they are.

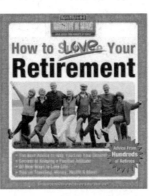

Why Retirement Rocks — Reason #337

Generally speaking, the complex organizational system itself does not do what it says it is doing. A complex system that doesn't work is invariably found to have evolved from a simple system that once worked. At this point, the complex system that no longer works cannot be patched up to make it work, regardless of the spin and smile presented by an expensive organizational consultant along with a silly flow chart. Fact is, the organization has to start from scratch — again beginning with a simple working system. If you work for such an organization, early retirement is the best option.

Why Retirement Rocks — Reason #338

New Year's Eve is much more fun when you are retired because you know that you can take a whole week to get over your hangover.

Why Retirement Rocks – Reason #339

With all the extra time you have you can rediscover the joy and challenge of team sports. The "teamwork"

required in team sports is something like the "teamwork" you used to have to indulge in at work — only far from being as brutal as at work. "One man alone can be pretty dumb sometimes," remarked Edward Abbey, "but for real bona fide stupidity, there ain't nothin' can beat teamwork."

Why Retirement Rocks – Reason #340

Retirement allows you to be in total control of your lifestyle — even if it is one that the Pope would likely frown upon.

Why Retirement Rocks — Reason #341

To the working stiffs of the world you can declare, "Somebody has to work — better you than me. I am retired and loving it!"

Why Retirement Rocks — Reason #342

The daily drudgery of making a living no longer has to keep your spouse and you from appreciating the sublime moments of life together.

Why Retirement Rocks – Reason #343

Infectious diseases can pose a serious risk in most workplaces. From the seasonal flu to respiratory diseases, a host of infectious diseases is responsible for worker illnesses, and in worse-case scenarios, even death. In a matter of a few hours, a sick person can pass an illness to a few or even hundreds of individuals. Being retired means that you no longer have to be exposed to all these diseases — including those mysterious ones that still don't have any names for them.

Why Retirement Rocks – Reason #344

If you harbor delusional fantasies of power and influence, retirement allows you the time to finally start keeping a journal of your thoughts and convictions that will provide invaluable insight for generations to come. Indeed, a priceless historical document in the making.

Why Retirement Rocks – Reason #345

When you were applying for your last job, the company's buzzwords were like symphony music to your unemployed ears. Based on what you were told, the company culture resembled Paradise. The employees' days were full of laughter, hugging, and working in the spirit of cooperation. What's more, the company's major goal was to make the world a better place for humanity. At the same time you were supposed to rapidly climb the corporate ladder and attain success and prosperity that others only dream of. In striking contrast, you soon realized that your company strongly believed in pulverizing its competition and then jacking up its prices to take any advantage of its customers. The company won contracts by intentionally underbidding. Then it closed the profit shortfall by doing extra shoddy work and grossly overcharging for upgrades. The only reason the company wasn't declared a criminal organization was because it was too hard to prove. Furthermore, your company didn't believe in paying taxes. Its extraordinary profits went toward making the shareholders even richer. Meanwhile your co-workers and you were stuck in the middle of the corporate ladder, being grossly underpaid, and living a life that had been stripped of all purpose and meaning. The good news is that retirement came to the rescue.

Why Retirement Rocks — Reason #346

Being retired means you no longer have to say this every morning: "I don't want to get up. I don't want to wait for the bus in the rain. I don't want to take orders from my boss. I don't want to go to stupid meetings."

Why Retirement Rocks — Reason #347

If you were a government worker before you retired, you no longer have to be the target of silly jokes, such as the one that starts with "Why did the government worker kill the snail?" and ends with "Because it was following him around all day."

Why Retirement Rocks – Reason #348

Retirement forces you to stop using the excuse that it is your job that is holding you back from doing the things that you have always wanted to do, such as learning how to ski.

Why Retirement Rocks – Reason #349

You get to spend more time with your loving spouse, teaching him or her how to play stimulating games that interest you.

Why Retirement Rocks — Reason #350

There are no more outrageously incongruent situations such as a person of your integrity fudging projects at work in an attempt to get them done quickly. To be sure, the results weren't always what you desired.

Why Retirement Rocks — Reason #351

Those workplace cubicles sure were a drag, weren't they? Virginia Woolf was right when she said, "What one really needs is simply a room of one's own. Stained coffee mugs, teetering stacks of books, and

all." Retirement is when you can enjoy that office (instead of a cubicle) of your own in your home, along with all the other great stuff that fits in a traditional office, particularly for someone retired. Peter Mayle also put things in proper perspective when he announced, "I'd rather live precariously in my own office than comfortably in somebody else's."

Why Retirement Rocks – Reason #352

During your working years starting time at work was the worst time of the workday and quitting time was the best time of the work day. In retirement, any time between what used to be your starting time of the day and your quitting time are great times of the day, such as when you go to the movies on a week-day afternoon.

Why Retirement Rocks – Reason #353

Being retired means that you can reserve the four months without an "r" in them — the ones best suited for outdoor activities — for your dog's and your own ultimate enjoyment. Try taking those four months as vacation time when you are working and see what happens. Indeed, I took two of those months (July and August) as unapproved vacation in 1980 which led to my getting fired from my Engineering job at the age of 41. It was not all that serious, however. Far from it! I semi-retired at that time, with a net worth of minus $30,000, never again to return to a regular job.

Why Retirement Rocks — Reason #354

After more than twenty-five years of staring out of an office window, wishing that you were someone else, somewhere else, you no longer have to do this. Once you are retired, you can be happy who you are — wherever you are.

Why Retirement Rocks — Reason #355

The great thing about being retired is that the minute you wake up in the morning you are already on the job, succeeding at the games of leisure and life, without anyone interfering with your game plan. For example, if you want to add to your rock collection, that's exactly what you get to do.

Why Retirement Rocks — Reason #356

Wherever you are, you can joyfully text message your former co-workers stating: "You know the Social Security that they keep deducting off your paycheck. Well, it's paying for my retirement, which I am truly enjoying to my heart's content. Thank you so much."

Why Retirement Rocks — Reason #357

You get to fill your days with healthy retirement activities — such as swimming, mountain biking, canoeing, and yoga — instead of unhealthy, stress-filled work activities such as meetings, boring tasks, and commuting. Incidentally, scientists at the University of Birmingham found that a group of cyclists aged between 55 and 79 who covered 180 miles a month and had cycled for 25 years had muscular strength, lung function, fitness levels, blood pressure, and immune systems far better than a group of sedentary 20- to 36-year-olds.

Why Retirement Rocks — Reason #358

The great writer Johann Wolfgang von Goethe once wisely advised, "One ought, every day at least, to hear a little song, read a good poem, see a fine picture, and, if it were possible, to speak a few reasonable words." Retirement allows you to do von Goethe proud.

Why Retirement Rocks — Reason #359

You can do what you want — when you want — anytime you want. As already said, society's rules that you are supposed to live by are not sacred. Your own truths, principles, and agreements are, however.

Why Retirement Rocks — Reason #360

Loud noise, including people talking too loudly, is one of the biggest complaints that employees have about the workplace. The great news is that in retirement you get to experience a lot more silence. As *Life's Secret Handbook* advises, "Silence — don't shun it. Embrace it. Silence is not only golden. It's the universal refuge. That's where you go for calm, peace, self-love, creativity, and energy."

Why Retirement Rocks — Reason #361

You get to find out that if you want to live a long and happy life, you must forget how old you are. Indeed, this gets more important the older you get.

Why Retirement Rocks – Reason #362

Retirement allows you to get your priorities straight and let everyone else know what they are. As the old saying wisely affirms, "No one on his or her death bed ever said, 'I wish I would have spent more time in the office.'"

Why Retirement Rocks – Reason #363

From retiree Bill Kalmar: "The best part [of retirement] is observing my neighbors go off to work in the morning knowing that that their day will be filled with jerks, brainless and endless meetings, jerks, vendor lunches where you hold your breath just waiting for the sales pitch until you regurgitate your pasta, more jerks, and the eventual company reorganization of the section that was just reorganized last month! Retirement? I'm lovin' it!"

Why Retirement Rocks — Reason #364

It's worth repeating. Retirement gives you the opportunity to write the book or books that you have always wanted to write. Here are ten more great benefits from writing a book:

- Writing is an effective way to add meaning to your life that you did not get from your job.
- It's a way to connect with the world.
- You get to influence and support others.
- Writing a book tells the world who you are.
- You can dedicate your book to someone special.
- It's a swell way to make money from your own creative efforts and feel much better for it.
- It makes you an authority on what you write about.
- Becoming a published author is a great personal achievement that can also lead to other satisfying experiences such as speaking engagements.
- A good book excites readers to self-discovery and making a difference in this world while you yourself make a difference.
- Being an author may be your true calling. Paradoxically, some retirees find their true life's calling after their main career of 40 years is over.

Why Retirement Rocks – Reason #365

Writing a goodbye letter for work in preparation for retirement is much more fun than work itself. Being the incurably romantic that you are, you can pen this resignation letter to your boss when you decide to take your surprise early retirement:

My Dearest Beloved Employer:

When we first met, there were hopes of great fortune for the two of us that would lead to a relationship filled with much love, life, light, and laughter.

Unfortunately, the blessings of good fortune have come to an end and there is no more future for the two of us. The Universe wasn't able to make a place for our hearts to meet. So it is with these few sad words that I bid Farewell.

Yours Forever and a Day,

Sheldon

No doubt your employer will find the letter so sweet and endearing that he will forego the 3-week or 6-week notice of resignation normally required. That will make for an even better retirement. Let the good times roll!

50 Bonus Reasons Why Retirement Rocks – and Work Sucks!

Why Retirement Rocks – Bonus Reason #1

You no longer have to feel like you are imprisoned for the eight or so hours a day that you are in the workplace.

Why Retirement Rocks – Bonus Reason #2

To be sure, the most useless computer tasks are invariably the most fun to do. In retirement you have all the time in the world to do these useless tasks, whenever and wherever you want.

Why Retirement Rocks – Bonus Reason #3

A grand promotion to the highest executive level always seemed to be your liberating ticket out of that two-bit dump of a cubicle that you labored in for way too many years. (A monkey's seat cushion has a better view than you had from your cubicle.) After you retired, you realized that is one star that you should never have hitched your wagon to.

Why Retirement Rocks – Bonus Reason #4

If you are a smoker, retirement means you no longer have to go outside in the cold to have a cigarette (or more) like you had to at the workplace. Better still, being retired and without a job will reduce the stress in your life. This may lead to your quitting smoking for good. That's what happened to me. In October 1980 I was fired from my Engineering job for taking too much vacation. Being without a real job (ever since) resulted in my quitting smoking in November 1982.

Why Retirement Rocks – Bonus Reason #5

Embarrassing situations that normally happen in the workplace are a thing of the past. Things such as wearing mismatched shoes to work, talking to someone and walking into the elevator door, coming out of the bathroom with toilet paper stuck to your shoe, and swearing at a co-worker after a phone call without realizing the co-worker is still on the line.

Why Retirement Rocks – Bonus Reason #6

You can join the "In Praise of Slowness Movement." Carl Honoré in his bestselling book *In Praise of Slowness: Challenging the Cult of Speed* advises, "The great benefit of slowing down is reclaiming the time and tranquility to make meaningful connections — with people, with culture, with work, with nature, with our own bodies and minds."

Why Retirement Rocks – Bonus Reason #7

You no longer have to deal with babbling bozo workers who have a social disorder that compels them to insert irrelevant stories and trite observations into other people's serious conversations.

Why Retirement Rocks – Bonus Reason #8

You have much more opportunity to satisfy your curiosity about the world. "Curiosity is the very basis of education," said Arnold Edinborough, "and if you tell me that curiosity killed the cat, I say only the cat died nobly." Indeed, a life without curiosity can lead to a boring life. It's the power of the curious mind that has made humans as creative and as advanced as we are today.

Why Retirement Rocks — Bonus Reason #9

Most workplace frustrations aren't worth contending with. According to the *Murphy's Law* book, if

anything is used to its full potential it will break. If you mess with something long enough, it will break too. What's more, anything is easier to take apart than to put together. Still more, whenever any mechanical contrivance fails, it will do so at the most inconvenient time possible. Who needs this? Viva la retirement!

Why Retirement Rocks — Bonus Reason #10

If you are ever in a hurry, you can hurry slowly and happily. Do keep in mind that the famous American historian Will Durant, who wrote *The Story of Civilization*, once said, "No man who is in a hurry is quite civilized."

Why Retirement Rocks – Bonus Reason #11

When a friend from out of town comes to visit unexpectedly, you can spend the whole day — even a whole week or a whole month — having coffee and indulging in other satisfying leisure activities with her.

Why Retirement Rocks – Bonus Reason #12

While alone you can indulge in truly interesting and satisfying leisure activities that connect you to all that is bigger than you. As *Life's Secret Handbook* states, "The Spirit of the Universe will be in concert with you when you are in concert with the Spirit of the Universe."

Why Retirement Rocks – Bonus Reason #13

Being retired means that you no longer have to work in a so-called "bullshit job." David Graeber, an anthropologist at the London School of Economics, argues in his 2018 book *Bullshit Jobs* that the existence of meaningless jobs does societal harm. He contends that over half of societal work is pointless, which becomes psychologically destructive when paired with a work ethic that associates work with self-worth. Surprisingly, these bullshit jobs are prevalent in the private sector with even many middle managers, leadership professionals, performance managers, in-house magazine journalists, leisure coordinators, lobbyists, corporate lawyers, telemarketers, and public relations specialists working in these useless jobs. In short, the best way to avoid these useless jobs is to be retired.

Why Retirement Rocks – Bonus Reason #14

If you are like a lot of people, getting that first pension check once you retire will be a bigger thrill and will make you happier than you were when you received the first pay check from your first job.

Why Retirement Rocks – Bonus Reason #15

During your working days, when you were starting to have a good time, this meant that you were doing your job wrong. On the other hand, during retirement, when you are starting to have a good time, this means that you are doing things right.

Why Retirement Rocks – Bonus Reason #16

Abraham Lincoln once proclaimed, "My father taught me to work, but not to love it. I never did like to work, and I don't deny it. I'd rather read, tell stories, crack jokes, talk, laugh — anything but work." The great news is that retirement is suited for reading, telling stories, cracking jokes, talking, laughing — anything but working.

Why Retirement Rocks — Bonus Reason #17

You and your spouse realize that "being on purpose" does not require a job or a career — just individual creativity, personal freedom, and leisure activities that enrich you." Pay particular attention to the leisure activities. "If you are losing your leisure, look out," warned Logan Pearsall Smith. "You are losing your soul."

Why Retirement Rocks — Bonus Reason #18

No enchanting moment lasts forever. Retirement is great for being able to savor that moment while it is still there. This is particularly true if you take up knitting. "The best thing about knitting is its slowness," says Bernadette Murphy, author of *Zen and The Art of Knitting*. "It is so slow that we see the beauty inherent in every tiny act that makes up a sweater. So slow that we know the project is not going to get finished today — it may not get finished for many months or longer — and that allows us to make our peace with the unresolved nature of life. We slow down as we knit."

Why Retirement Rocks — Bonus Reason #19

You have more time to do things that satisfy your wild side — romantically or otherwise!

Why Retirement Rocks — Bonus Reason #20

The idea of daylight savings time was first thought of by Benjamin Franklin and then advocated seriously in 1907 by London builder William Willett who said, "Everyone appreciates the long, light evenings. Everyone laments their shortage as Autumn approaches; and everyone has given utterance to regret that the clear, bright light of an early morning during Spring and Summer months is so seldom seen or used."

As a retiree, if you forget to set your clocks ahead or behind one hour for daylight savings time, happily there are no consequences. For workers there can be.

Why Retirement Rocks – Bonus Reason #21

Bo Bennett described a résumé as "a written exaggeration of only the good things a person has

done in the past, as well as a wish list of the qualities a person would like to have." No doubt creating a great résumé while you were looking for work was always a chore. The great news is that after a few years of being retired, you will still know what "resume" means but you will have completely forgotten what "résumé" means.

Why Retirement Rocks – Bonus Reason #22

In a November 2016 *Forbes* article about the top-10 reasons why people hate their jobs, the number 4 reason was: "Their immediate supervisor is a tyrant, unqualified for their job, or both." From your retirement day onward you no longer have to deal with the hot-headed know-nothing boss who used her arrogance to mask her total incompetence. To be sure, she ruined every meeting with her toxic personality. What's more, every project she interfered with turned into total failure, which she blamed on your hard working co-workers and you. Viva la retirement.

Why Retirement Rocks — Bonus Reason #23

Bob Black in his book *Workers of the World, Relax* warned, "You are what you do. If you do boring, stupid, monotonous work, chances are you'll end up boring, stupid, and monotonous." To be sure, if you did boring, stupid, monotonous work at your last job, retirement is a great time to indulge in some exciting and self-fulfilling activities and to correct any negative consequences of having done that boring, stupid, monotonous work for so many years.

Why Retirement Rocks — Bonus Reason #24

Things that your spouse and you put off in your youth can now be pursued with zeal.

Why Retirement Rocks – Bonus Reason #25

You will discover by speaking to other individuals that retirement is not necessarily for everyone and that your intense joy in the experience is not shared by every retiree. This makes retirement in itself even more special to happy retirees such as you.

Why Retirement Rocks – Bonus Reason #26

Retirement parties are great even when they aren't your own. This is particularly true when it's your boss's retirement party and you know he won't be back in your workplace ever again. You get to give him a cheap cheesy gift to show your true appreciation for his dubious years of service.

Why Retirement Rocks — Bonus Reason #27

You were given three special gifts when you were born: The gift of life, the gift of love, and the gift of laughter. Retirement is the best time of your life to share these gifts with the rest of the world — and have the rest of the world play merrily with you while you joyfully pursue your leisure activities.

Why Retirement Rocks — Bonus Reason #28

You get to visit your grandchildren more often.

Why Retirement Rocks – Bonus Reason #29

You can laugh at nothing in particular and be silly more often. There can be great health benefits from this. Norman Cousins used laughter as an amazing mind-power cure to recover from a diagnosed terminal illness which he described in his bestselling book, *Anatomy of an Illness*. He spent months watching hilarious

movies like those of the Marx Brothers. As a result, he literally laughed himself out of his disease. Even his doctors agreed that his mental state was the crucial determinate in his overcoming his "incurable" illness.

Why Retirement Rocks – Bonus Reason #30

You get to discover that there is little evidence that working life is better than retirement life. Indeed, if you think otherwise, you can write a book called *The Joy of NOT Being Retired: 365 Reasons Why Work Rocks — and Retirement Sucks!* Make sure that you also include *50 Bonus Reasons Why Work Rocks — and Retirement Sucks* for a total of 415 Reasons!

Why Retirement Rocks — Bonus Reason #31

You also get to discover that the key to a happy retirement has little to do with what financial advisors tell you and more with what holistic lifestyle planners tell you. Handling leisure is the important thing. In this regard Roman statesman, orator, and philosopher Marcus Tullius Cicero remarked, "Leisure consists in all those virtuous activities by which a man grows morally, intellectually, and spiritually. It is that which makes a life worth living."

Why Retirement Rocks — Bonus Reason #32

Whenever you are doing something difficult or time-consuming, you can ask yourself what would happen if you don't do it. In the event the answer is nothing, or next to nothing, you can stop doing it. The workplace doesn't give you this option.

Why Retirement Rocks – Bonus Reason #33

Of course there is no guarantee that retirement will bring you happiness. But neither is there a guarantee that work will bring you happiness. As Clint Eastwood once pronounced, "If you want a guarantee, buy a toaster." Keeping this in mind, you will get to use that toaster in a much more leisurely fashion when you retire than when you are working.

Why Retirement Rocks – Bonus Reason #34

Brien's Law states, "At some time in the life cycle of virtually every shoddy organization, its ability to succeed in spite of itself runs out." (I worked for such an organization and quit two months before the inevitable happened.) Early retirement is an intelligent strategy for avoiding this inevitable messy organizational situation, including a hostile workplace mob angry at everyone around it, everything around it, and even itself.

Why Retirement Rocks – Bonus Reason #35

Vicki Baum said that "There are short-cuts to happiness, and dancing is one of them." Being retired means that your spouse and you can take this shortcut to happiness practically any time you want. Don't be

afraid of feeling like mere fools for doing this. "We're fools whether we dance or not, so we might as well dance," according to a not-so-famous Japanese proverb.

Why Retirement Rocks – Bonus Reason #36

You can write a blog about the joy of being retired with the chance that you may be chosen to star in a documentary as an example of the types of risky things people should not do if they want to truly enjoy retirement to the fullest.

Why Retirement Rocks – Bonus Reason #37

You have the opportunity to prove that the only way of discovering the limits of the possible is to venture a little ways past them into the impossible. As an unknown wise person pointed out, "If you aren't living on the edge, you're taking up way too much space."

Why Retirement Rocks – Bonus Reason #38

Particularly if you have a good pension, you get to experience that the money you enjoy spending frivolously is money well spent. All things considered, it's better, in the words of Henry David Thoreau, "to live rich than to die rich." Several other wise people have warned us about the folly of not enjoying our money. "To die rich," stated spiritual teacher Jiddu Krishnamurti, "is to have lived in vain." Errol Flynn declared, "Any man who has $10,000 left when he dies is a failure." Not to be outdone, Thomas Fuller pronounced, "He is not fit for riches who is afraid to use them."

Why Retirement Rocks – Bonus Reason #39

You no longer have to face the dim possibility that the final humiliation you will face is when you die at your workplace screaming at your boss. *Life's Secret Handbook* cautions, "Death often comes at a bad time." Nevertheless, there are a few ways of dying in retirement that are much more dignified and even much more delightful.

Why Retirement Rocks – Bonus Reason #40

In retirement you can take up being a comedian which was always your true calling. Start your comedy roll

by blurting, "Why don't most cannibals like comedians?" and then answer, "Because they taste funny." Be a bit careful, however. American humorist Will Rogers warned, "Everything is changing. People are taking their comedians seriously and the politicians as a joke."

Why Retirement Rocks — Bonus Reason #41

Tim Gould once said, "I've been promoted to middle management. I never thought I'd sink so low." The problem with working in a middle management position is that you don't have the sole authority to approve anything important. Sure, you have the authority to reject all sorts of ideas from subordinates. But if you don't do that dubious task, there is nothing for you to do. If you have just retired after being employed in middle management for many years, what a relief this must be.

Why Retirement Rocks — Bonus Reason #42

Life's Secret Handbook ends with these words:

> "Don't ever grow up.
> Be forever young in Spirit.
> Spend your entire life in the most inspirational, adventurous, and creative way possible."

Retirement is the time to put this remarkable advice to great use.

Why Retirement Rocks – Bonus Reason #43

In retirement, there are no serious consequences when you declare, "The heck with 'teamwork.' I never did like that word — or the two words from which it originates." Fact is, the truly creative people of this world prize individuality and independence — and care little about teamwork.

Why Retirement Rocks – Bonus Reason #44

You have all the time in the world to accomplish a task — regardless of what it is. Even so, don't take too much time with just one simple task. Retiree John Burrough remarked, "I still find each day too short for all the thoughts I want to think, all the walks I want to take, all the books I want to read, and all the friends I want to see."

Why Retirement Rocks – Bonus Reason #45

According to a Turkish proverb, "There is no right way to do a wrong thing." Retirement allows you the time to read a lot, to reflect a lot, and to realize that there is no right way to do any of these things:

- to be a workaholic
- to be an extreme consumer
- to be a perfectionist
- to live life properly without enjoying leisure
- to live forever

Why Retirement Rocks – Bonus Reason #46

You no longer have a Daytimer because you forget to look in it after making an entry. You just do things whenever you want to do them.

Why Retirement Rocks – Bonus Reason #47

You have much more time and opportunity to reactivate old friendships and cultivate new ones with people of all ages.

Why Retirement Rocks – Bonus Reason #48

As already stated, freedom is when you can get up in the morning when you want to get up; go to sleep when you want to go to sleep; and in the interval, work and play at the things you want to work and play at — all at your own pace. Retirement allows you the opportunity to attain this freedom.

Why Retirement Rocks – Bonus Reason #49

American congressman, diplomat, and author Samuel Sullivan Cox some time ago wrote: "How she felt when he kissed her — like a tub of roses swimming in honey, cologne, nutmeg, and blackberries." No doubt things exploded from this point on! This woman — no matter who she was — felt much more ecstatic than this when she retired.

Why Retirement Rocks – Bonus Reason #50

The older you get, the more amazed you are about the many ways you can enjoy yourself while being retired.

ABOUT THE AUTHOR

Photograph by Greg Gazin

Ernie J. Zelinski is an international best-selling author, prosperity life coach, innovator, speaker, and unconventional career expert. Ernie's two life-changing retirement books — *How to Retire Happy, Wild, and Free* (over 390,000 copies sold) and *The Joy of Not Working* (over 310,000 copies sold) — have helped hundreds of thousands of people experience personal growth and create a happy and satisfying retirement.

Ernie has negotiated over 111 book deals with publishers in 29 countries for his various creative works — which have been published in 22 languages and have sold over 1,000,000 copies.

Ernie speaks on the topics of retirement, unconventional career success, and creativity. He recently made keynote speeches about *The Joy of Not Working* to over 2,000 executives and scholars at the National Turkish Congress on Quality (Kalder) in Istanbul, Turkey and to 1,200 career experts at the National Career Development Association convention in Orlando, Florida.

Contact Ernie about buying quantity copies of his books for your organization or about speaking at your event by email at vipbooks@telus.net or phone him at 780-434-9202.